ON THE ROAD WITH ABRAHAM
TRUST FOR THE JOURNEY

BY: ANDREA LENNON

True Vine Publishing
Conway, Arkansas

Copyright © 2023 by Andrea Lennon

Printed by Kindle Direct Publishing, a division of Amazon Publishing

ISBN- 9798876377432

All rights reserved.

No part of this book may be used or reproduced in any manner whatsoever without written permission, except in the case of brief quotations embedded in critical articles or reviews. Requests for permission should be sent by email to andrea@andrealennonministry.org.

Printed in the United States of America

All Scripture quotations, unless otherwise indicated, are taken from the Holy Bible, Christian Standard Bible®, Copyright © 2017 by Holman Bible Publishers. Used by permission. Christian Standard Bible® and CSB® are federally registered trademarks of Holman Bible Publishers.

Scripture Quotations marked NIV have been taken from the New International Version®, NIV®. Copyright © 1973, 1978, 1984, 2011 by Biblica, Inc.™. Used by permission of Zondervan. All rights reserved worldwide. www.zondervan.com. The "NIV" and "New International Version" are trademarks registered in the United States Patent and Trademark Office by Biblica, Inc.™.

Cover art by Mae Joy Creative.

Author photos by Kelsey Blackmon.

Additional copies of this book can be ordered at www.andrealennonministry.org or www.amazon.com.

CONTENTS

Preface...	7
INTRODUCTION - Andrea's Journey................................	9
Chapter 1 - God, Can I Trust You?.....................................	13
Chapter 2 - Hard Times Lead to a Choice........................	27
Chapter 3 - Trusting God Leads to Intimacy with God....	41
Chapter 4 - God-Sized Moments......................................	55
Chapter 5 - Questions and Doubts...................................	67
Chapter 6 - The God Who Sees...	81
Chapter 7 - Marked by God...	93
Chapter 8 - Little by Little..	107
Chapter 9 - Grace in the Moment.....................................	119
Epilogue - By Faith..	132
About the Author..	134
True Vine Publishing Resources......................................	135
Bibliography...	138

Dedication

I dedicate this book to my mom and dad. You gave me a beautiful life and space to thrive. You encourage me, love me, and help me. When I think of people God placed in my life who demonstrate faith and trust in God's plan, you are at the top of the list. I will never get over the grace of God. I love you.

Forever grateful,
Andrea

PREFACE

Welcome to our study on the life of Abraham! I am excited to begin this adventure together. Throughout this study, we will see God's plan unfold in the life of Abraham, which will lead us to dive deep into the topic of trusting God. Whether we're female or male, young or old, new or experienced in walking with God—all of us can learn from the way Abraham and God journeyed together.

When we look at the world, it's discouraging to see everything that's going wrong. We can focus on all the bad news and on all our question marks about the future. But we can also choose to focus on the fact that God is at work. He is moving forward with His big, eternal plan, and in the midst of that, He meets us where we are and wants to use us!

The two main themes in this book are faith in God and trust in God. Faith and trust go hand in hand because they lead to surrender. If we don't trust in God and who He is, we're not going to fully put our faith in God. We will hold back and try to stay in control. This truth invites us to check our hearts. If we don't really want to live by faith, then we don't really have to trust God at a deeper level. The good news is that if we want to step out in faith and trust…there is a faith adventure waiting for us!

But here is the deal. We can't stir up our emotions and just decide, "I'm going to be full of faith and trust!" No. We cultivate faith by letting go of control while expecting that God has better plans for us, and is preparing the road ahead of us. And we cultivate trust by walking down that road with obedience and spiritual focus, especially in seasons of the unknown.

As a note, the chapters in this book are built on a "His Journey" and an "Our Journey" section, with parallel points between Abraham's life and our lives. We have a lot to cover, so grab your Bible, a journal, some friends, and let's dig into God's Word!

Sweet friend, it's going to be an adventure, and I'm glad you're here for it.

Much love!
Andrea

Introduction,
ANDREA'S JOURNEY

"Expect great things from God. Attempt great things for God."
William Carey [1]

In March 2020, I had the privilege of speaking in my hometown of Conway, Arkansas. I traveled a lot to speak for my ministry, and had dozens of upcoming speaking commitments, but whenever I got to speak in my hometown it was extra special. This time it was at "Transformed," an event for friends and family involved with an addiction recovery program. And this group, more than most, pushed me to a place of vulnerability because they had chosen to be vulnerable themselves. It's easy to pretend we have it all together, but this was a place where I could tell it was safe to be real. Surrounded by moms, sisters, friends, and family members who had been impacted by addiction, there was a freedom for me not to hide my own problems and struggles. I had planned to talk about Romans 12:2 and how it says, "Do not conform to the pattern of this world...." My whole day had been crazy, and hurrying to the event, I asked God to give me the words to speak.

At one point, I opened my mouth, and something came out that I hadn't planned to say. It stayed with me in the months to follow. I said, "I want to come to a place in life where all of my eggs are in God's basket." If you're from the South, you know the actual saying is, "Don't put your eggs in one basket." But that night, I knew the actual best thing I could do was to put all of my eggs in God's basket, to choose His plan over my own. I realized I didn't want to come up with a great plan and ask God to bless it; I didn't want to gauge God's goodness by my own success or happiness. It was an epiphany to hear myself say that, no matter what happened, I wanted to trust God.

And that was good because the next day Arkansas shut down from the pandemic. All of my speaking events for an entire year were canceled. Every single one. All the activities of life and ministry came to a screeching halt. To top it off, I was transitioning my ministry from an LLC to a nonprofit, so the ministry was not eligible for financial assistance. This led to a hard look at my ministry plan and our personal finances with my husband.

I went to my prayer closet and spent months with the Lord. I realized I was tired and overextended. I needed a reset, and in the most unusual and unexpected way, I was going to get one. While my circumstances had changed, God had not. I knew God was giving me a real-life chance to put all of my eggs in His basket, leaving me to watch Him supply exactly what I needed.

Out of my time with the Lord came the idea for the Girl on the Go Community. It started with a private Facebook group that I could jump on each day and teach God's Word and interact with others. My usual ministry involved live speaking events at women's conferences, women's retreats, and community events for nonprofit organizations. The lockdown meant live events were on hold. In the isolation, I had it in my heart to connect with other women in an online community where we could keep growing and learning together. Honestly, I had wanted to start that type of community prior to the pandemic, but I never had the time. For the first time in a long time, I had plenty of time! During the first few months of the pandemic, I taught several different Bible studies in the Girl on the Go Community. Even once the lockdowns lessened, and speaking events were allowed again, the online community was too special to close down. When it came time for the next Bible study, I decided to study the life of Abraham. I loved the idea of going back to the beginning of God's story and seeing how God called Abraham to a life of faith. So I started preparing by researching (What was the culture in his hometown? What do historians say about Canaan?) and studying the Bible itself.

Each day I pored over Abraham's journey. It amazed me how much I could relate to him! There was so much to share with the women I was teaching online but also so much that was relevant for any believer, every believer. As I studied Abraham's life, I started wondering if there was more that God was calling me to explore. Little did I know it would lead to this book!

There's a saying: "Write what you know." But I wasn't drawn to the story of Abraham because trust is my strong point! Honestly, I fight daily to let go of control and follow God's plan. I wrote this book for the woman who wants to trust God, but —like me—is sometimes terrified at the thought of it. What fascinated me was that, even with his own fears and crises, Abraham still trusted God. I saw how he left his old, familiar life to follow God's invitation...and then he kept on following. And kept on following. That's why we can learn so much from his life. Centuries later, we have our own chance to impact the world for God's glory. But to do that, we have to let go of our own doubts, plans, and comfort levels. We have to be open to a fresh move of God in our lives!

Writing this book led to more soul searching than I expected. *What is my role in my life? What is God's role in my life? Where does God's role end and my role begin? Is there a formula for success?* If you have followed my ministry and read my books, especially *God in the Window*, you know that control has been an ongoing struggle for me. But, by God's grace, I am making progress! What I'm learning is that faith is more than just surrendering control and then waiting passively on God. It's learning to actually enjoy the steps God has prepared for me. Surrender is giving up; faith is leaning in.

There's a phrase I use as a sort of test for my motives and actions: "Is this **to** God, **with** God, **for** God, and **through** God?"
- To God: meaning for His glory and His praise, not for my own.
- With God: meaning in partnership with God, not in my own independence.
- For God: meaning focused on His kingdom, not my own.
- Through God: meaning with His power, not my own.

While studying the life of Abraham, I saw times when he made decisions that were to, with, for, and through God—and times when he tried to do it all on his own. One of the most challenging things about writing this book was that there is so much material on Abraham. For example, the story of Ruth in the Bible is four chapters, and focuses on a few weeks, maybe months of her life. In Genesis, the story of Abraham has about twelve chapters, and focuses on about twenty-five years of his life. I saw over and over how Abraham's faith in God was tested, and how he failed and triumphed along the way. And that gave me hope. If Abraham could trust God with his life, family, and legacy, I could do the same. If he could give up control, one decision at a time, so could I.

The big question we see over and over again in Abraham's story is this: God, can I trust You? And, honestly, that's a question for all of us. ***God, can I trust You?***

I'm so excited to explore this question with you. I can't wait to see what God has in store for all of us.

Chapter 1

God, Can I Trust You?

Even though it took place thousands of years ago, the story of Abraham is close to the heart of our story as believers in Jesus Christ. As we study the life of Abraham, we gain beautiful truths and rich knowledge that can be applied to our lives.

What I love about Abraham and his story is that it's real. It's filled with God-sized moments where God showed up and spoke. But it's also filled with sin and struggle. In Abraham's journey, we see both faith and fear.

All of these realities lead to a story that is relatable for us. It's not pristine and clean; it's just real and honest. I'm grateful for that, and grateful that Abraham's story is captured in the Word of God. As we see the God-sized moments in his life, it challenges us to trust God more, and to expect some God-sized moments in our own lives. And those difficult moments in Abraham's life? Well, we can learn from those, too.

His Journey

Are you ready to dig into the life of Abraham? Before we start our study, let's settle an important detail. Is his name Abram or Abraham—or both?

A man named Abram is introduced in Genesis 11, listed as a descendent of Noah, who was a descendent of Adam. The genealogy, or family record, set the stage for one man, who would establish one family, which would lead to one nation. (Spoiler: God was directing every detail because Jesus eventually came from this family!)

The name Abram means, "The father is exalted."[2] The name Abraham means, "Father of a multitude."[3] Abram's name change pointed to one of his biggest faith opportunities ever—the opportunity to trust God with his descendants.

Throughout our study, we will see how God continually invited Abram into a trusting relationship and how the change of his name represented a step of faith. And while the names of Abram and Abraham can be used interchangeably, we will respect God's ongoing work and use the name corresponding to the passage we are studying. So, for now, we will call this man Abram. Later, we will call him Abraham.

When we meet Abram, he was married to a woman named Sarai, whose name would also later change. Sarai played a major role in Abram's story; these two were inseparable in their journey. Both of them learned about faith in God and trust in God.

I can't wait to dig into this story with you. Let's get started in Genesis 12. There we'll discover four key points when it comes to Abram's introduction into the story of God. And then those four key points will lead us to our transforming truth: trust is rooted in God.

1. God Showed Up

Let's get to know Abram. Where was he from? What was his purpose in life? What did he struggle with? Why would God pick him?

The Bible tells us that Abram was originally from Ur which scholars think was located in modern-day Iraq.[4] Ur was a rich port city and center for international trade, boasting conveniences like libraries and running water.[5] The people worshiped a host of gods in shrines and temples across the city, so Abram's choice to follow only one God may have seemed strange to his family and friends.[6]

In Genesis 11:31, we see that Abram and his family—his father, wife, and nephew—left Ur and settled in Haran.[7] Scholars think Haran was located in modern-day Turkey,[8] in an area with wide pastures and abundant water.[9] For a family with many animals, Haran was probably a great place to live.

Abram was married to Sarai, and from the beginning of the story we are told that Sarai was barren. There were no children and there was no hope for children. There was a nephew named Lot who we will get to know, and a father named Terah, but he died before the story really got started.

Although there are some archaeological hints of names in Abram's family tree, we don't find Abram's story recorded outside of the Bible.[10] It's not surprising, considering his life as a nomad and the fact he lived during the Bronze Age. Imagine living during a time when clay tablets were carried on the backs of donkeys, and social media was not a thing. An anonymous life, with no record left of someone's existence, was normal. Interestingly, God was about to create lineage out of unknown lineage. For hundreds of years after, being a descendant of this man shaped a person's culture, language, and very identity.

Still, in our modern age, it's easy to assume that the lack of strong archaeological evidence counts as evidence against Abram's existence. But here's what I love about Abram's story. God often works through the least likely people to make a way for His people. Abram had resources and he had a family, but he was not royalty or a conqueror mentioned in the clay tablets in Ur's libraries.[11]

One day, God showed up and spoke to this unlikely man.

The Lord said to Abram: Go from your land, your relatives, and your father's house to the land that I will show you.
Genesis 12:1

Wow! Talk about a big moment in Abram's life. He was doing normal things in Haran when God initiated an encounter with him. It wasn't Abram's idea to follow God on some adventure across the Middle East. Abram didn't even know where he was supposed to go. All Abram knew was to go to the place God would show him.

This reminds us of three important truths that set the stage for God's work in Abram's life and our lives, too:
- **God is Sovereign.** God is in charge of the people and things He has created.[12]
- **God is Providential.** God is always working, directing the events of life.
- **God is Purposeful.** God is working according to a plan that He has determined.

The encounter between God and Abram was setting the stage for the future. Abram was learning about God, and Abram was going to see how God faithfully acted. Abram had the chance to place his trust in the One True God. Doing that would mean uprooting his life and family to follow God's instruction.

In verse one, God was specific with Abram: "Go...to the land that I will show you" (Genesis 12:1). God had a plan and the plan was fixed in God's heart. God showed up, and as God showed up, God made a promise for Abram's life.

2. *God Made a Promise*

What was the promise God had for Abram and his family? Hang on, because this was a BIG one! As you read the promise, think about what it was like for Abram to hear this news from God.

I will make you into a great nation, I will bless you, I will make your name great, and you will be a blessing. I will bless those who bless you, I will curse anyone who treats you with contempt, and all the peoples on earth will be blessed through you.
Genesis 12:2-3

Now, that was a big promise! Abram was going to have a descendant. Not just that, he was going to have lots of descendants. At that moment in Abram's life, do you think he would have dreamed as big as the promise God made? Do you think Abram would have come up with that kind of plan for his life, family, and legacy?

Remember, Abram's wife was barren. But God said, "I will make you into a great nation. I will make your name great! You will be a blessing." This was a promise that probably seemed impossible to Abram. But Abram did not have the big picture perspective we have today. We know that God was going to build a nation of people through Abram, and that the Messiah would come from that family. But, in the early stages of the promise, it had to seem unbelievable, even ridiculous.

One thing Abram was going to learn was that God was a promise-making and a promise-keeping God. Way back at the very beginning of God's unfolding story of redemption, the thread of the impossible being possible was set into motion. The promise God made to Abram required faith to believe it and trust to walk it out. It was an impossible promise; Abram couldn't make it happen with his strength or with his resources; it would take a move of God.

God showed up. God made a promise to Abram. How would Abram respond?

3. Abram Showed Up

We find the next part of Abram's story in Genesis 12:4-6. I love that the passage is punchy and filled with lots of details—all of which are important. Abram's response to God sets up the rest of the story, with clues that would change his future.

So Abram went, as the Lord had told him, and Lot went with him. Abram was seventy-five years old when he left Haran. He took his wife, Sarai, his nephew Lot, all the possessions they had accumulated, and the people they had acquired in Haran, and they set out for the land of Canaan. When they came to the land of Canaan, Abram passed through the land to the site of Shechem, at the oak of Moreh. (At that time the Canaanites were in the land.)
Genesis 12:4-6

How did Abram respond to God showing up? Abram showed up! Abram left Haran as the Lord had told him. Period. Abram responded in faith. Abram responded in obedience. He got up from the place where he was, and he went to the place that God would show him.

We are going to get to know this place: Canaan. We're going to walk the length and breadth of the land with Abram. We'll watch God faithfully promise the land to Abram, and we will see Abram make mistakes while living in the land. Ultimately, God and Abram will enter into a covenant in the heart of this land, securing a future not only for Abram but also for his descendants.

Showing up for Abram meant believing God for a future Abram could not produce or provide for himself. To do that, Abram had to let go of his plans and embrace God's plan. All of this was happening in "real-time" for Abram. He was hearing from God and responding to God by faith—and one step at a time.

So, back to Genesis 12. Once Abram was in Canaan, he traveled through the land, and God appeared to Abram with one more important piece of information. How would Abram respond to God? How would the encounter change Abram's life? How would it change the lives of others?

4. Abram Worshiped God

Imagine the scene with me. Abram was living an anonymous life when God appeared to him in Haran. The encounter led Abram on a journey to an unfamiliar place called Canaan. Abram had no child. His wife was barren. He was a stranger in a land where the Canaanite tribes were living. This unlikely man with an anonymous identity would eventually become the Father of a Nation. Abram had been unknown but he would be well-known for generations to come. And not only would he be famous; he would be key to God's promise. It was against that backdrop that the Lord showed up and extended one more promise.

> *The Lord appeared to Abram and said, "To your offspring I will give this land." So he built an altar there to the Lord who had appeared to him.*
> *Genesis 12:7*

Talk about a big day! Not only was Abram going to have descendants, the descendants would get the land of Canaan. So what did Abram do? He could have asked questions. He could have run away. Instead, Abram worshiped God.

By building an altar, Abram was saying, "God, I choose to believe you. I surrender to Your future for me." He wasn't fighting the plan of God; he was responding to it in his own way. Abram's heart was open to receiving that promise for the descendants and the land, however unlikely it may have seemed as a nomad with no children. The promise was for the future, but it was also a reality that he was receiving at that moment because Abram was in the presence of God.

Abram and his descendants had a secure future with a certain identity. They were going to be God's chosen people. They were going to be the apple of God's eye. They were going to be the people that God would provide for and protect. God would talk with them personally. He would appear to them, and guide them. Of course, God would redirect them when they sinned. God was going to work miracles in and through these people. This commitment was firm in God's heart and mind, and every step of the way God was going to provide exactly what the people would need, and it all started with the promise of a son and the provision of some land. But the journey for Abram was going to be long. And while the future was secured, it was not "snap your fingers and make it happen" secured. The journey would be filled with ups and downs and twists and turns. Along the way, Abram was going to learn about faith and trust as God guided him. Just like He guides us.

Our Journey

I was flying to speak at a conference. I'd just gotten settled in my chair when someone asked if I could switch seats with them. No problem. I traded seats, opened my conference notes, and started preparing.

"Excuse me," said my new seat neighbor. "I was curious about your notes, and the word 'hope....'" It turned out that she hadn't planned to be on this flight at all, but her business plans changed. I hadn't planned to be in that seat, and yet there we both were. On that plane ride, I got to share about my notes and the conference. But most importantly, I got to share how I find hope in God, despite our crazy world.

For me, I see God in all that. He can change her plans and my seat. He can prepare my heart with a message of hope, and prompt her to ask about it. God is always doing more than we know. I often say, "God is not doing one thing; He is doing so many things!"

In my life, I've seen time and time again that God initiates encounters and we have the chance to respond in faith. What have you seen God do in yours?

-Andrea

I love that God is always working in and through our lives. Just like Abram had encounters with God, we have encounters with God. God had a journey for Abram and God has a journey for us. So let's take the truths we learned from Genesis 12:1-9 in His Journey and apply them to Our Journey.

1. God Shows Up

When you look back, can you think of examples of when God showed up in your life? Where did He provide for you or protect you? We can look back and list example after example of God showing up in history as well as in our own faith journeys. It's like going to the same national park every year...and yet taking new paths each time. When we look back we see familiar sights. God always shows up, and God always has a plan. And yet we're always going to have new adventures; every day we're taking a new path through the canyon of grace.

In Abram's Journey, we looked at three important truths: **God is sovereign, providential, and purposeful.** God is working according to His plan, even when we don't know what His plan is. So, another thing we have in common with Abram is the fact that the journey is unpredictable! We never know what adventures God has for us next, and we never know when He'll next show up.

I like to divide moments where God shows up into big encounters and little encounters. Big encounters are those stake-in-the-ground moments that shape us and our story. The defining moments—good and hard—that we think of when we look at the course of our lives. The moment God nudged you towards a career choice, or the day you gave your testimony and were baptized. Or maybe the time you found out your parents were getting a divorce, and God was the only one who listened to you grieve. A youth retreat where you met Jesus, or a marriage retreat that saved your marriage. Those are moments that shaped you, and you know God was with you through it all. Big, bold encounters.

The little encounters are the day-in-and-day-out ways that God is doing way more than we know. When He sent just the right person at just the right time to say just the right thing, and you only realized it later. Maybe a song on the radio was exactly what you needed to get you through that tough conversation at work. A breath of divine patience when dealing with a screaming toddler. Or that verse in the Bible that you have read one hundred times that spoke to you in a fresh way. Little, subtle encounters.

Just like God showed up in Abram's life, He shows up in ours. He has a plan that is individual and unique for each of us. He also lines everything up for that plan to happen. He doesn't expect us to get ourselves ready before He's willing to meet with us; He meets us where we are. Whether we're focused or distracted, faithful or sinful, thriving or struggling- He meets us. He has these God-moments planned for us throughout our days, so that we can connect with His heart and are reminded of who He is.

In our world, God is working daily. We just have to open our eyes to see it! That's why it's important to start our day by talking to God, because then we can see things differently throughout the hours of our day. Starting our day with God helps us to be sensitive to what's happening around us. It helps us learn to live in that rhythm of trust and faith, instead of waiting for once-in-a-lifetime encounters. If we could pull back the curtain spiritually, and see the ways God is working, it would blow our minds. Of course, we can't see what's happening the way He does, so we just keep trucking on. Not all stories finish with a neat and tidy bow. We may not know the outcome of the 'God moments'—a talk with a stranger, the chance to see something start, a faith jump. But God knows the outcome. And He is faithful to His word and the promises He made to us.

God has always been and He will always be. Your life, and my life, begins with God. God's creative design gives everything and everyone their context for existing. Our lives are defined by His love and His pursuit of us. God faithfully shows up on the landscape of our lives and moves according to His plan.

Here is the bottom line: God is directing our lives according to His plan. God is faithful to intervene in our lives at the right time, in the right way, and with the right people. When God shows up in our lives, the encounters reveal the plan He has for us (or at least part of it!). We don't have to try to control our lives. Our lives were meant to revolve around God—the question is whether we will choose that. Daily we can live **to** God, **with** God, **for** God, and **through** God.

2. God Makes a Promise

Humans are just so limited by our thinking and our frame of reference. We tend to think small. We tend to think safe. We tend to think compartmentalized. We tend to think about the temporary. We are finite, and so are our plans. God, on the other hand, is infinite. He is beyond what we can grasp or imagine. As a result, so are His plans. That's the beauty of God's individual and unique work in our lives.

The Bible is filled with God's faithful promises, both big, sweeping world-changing ones, and small, more intimate ones. Abram's story is recorded in the Old Testament, at the beginning of God revealing His plan to redeem the world. Anytime we study the Old Testament, we need to remember that the storyline is pointing to the coming of a Messiah, a Savior. The promise of a Messiah was God's good plan to bring humans back to Himself.

The very foundation of our faith has roots in Genesis 12. Hundreds of years after Abram was given the promise, Jesus came. He was a descendant of Abraham but also God Himself and He provided the only way for us to be saved from ourselves and our sins. As we think about our journeys, and the promises that God gives us, Jesus is in the middle of it!

The promise of a Messiah is huge, but that isn't the only promise in the Bible that affects us on a day-to-day basis. I could list dozens of promises we can proclaim about God's unending love and His commitment to us from the Old Testament alone. And then in the New Testament, we see so many promises come true in Jesus, as well as new ones that He made to all believers. God works through various ways but the Bible is the primary way He speaks. In 2 Peter 1:3, we read, "His divine power has given us everything required for life and godliness through the knowledge of him who called us by his own glory and goodness." That 'knowledge' leads to a personal intimate relationship with God through Jesus, who is a promise made, and a promise kept.

3. We Show Up

As the saying goes, 80% of success comes from just showing up. We want to show up for our own future,but we don't always know how. When God shows up in our lives, we have the choice to run from God or show up in faith.

When God shows up in your life, He's not going to leave you alone after that to try to figure out the next steps. He's already given you principles and promises in the Bible to guide you in following Him. Think about your current season of life, a huge question, or an upcoming choice. God may not tell you exactly which school or job to apply for (no matter how much you want Him to!), but He does give us directions. Instead of us hyper-focusing on a certain school or profession, God says that whatever we do, to do it for the glory of God (1 Corinthians 10:31). We may not have a specific word from God on whether we should move to Kenya, Taiwan, or Florida, but the Bible does tell us that He will be with us always, and to make disciples as we go (Matthew 28:19).

There's no perfect formula for making decisions. We can't pigeonhole God's will. But the Bible is full of promises that we can use as guide rails in choices like who to marry or where to live. Are we making choices with a pure heart? Are we acting in humility instead of selfish ambition and pride (Philippians 2:3)? Are we asking for wisdom as we go (James 1:5)?

A simple question for us to ask—looking at our choices—is: *"What does a faith-filled life look like for me in this situation?"* That's when we look at the fruit of the Spirit. God can work through circumstances and people, opening doors and closing doors to lead us in what He has for us. Have you searched God's Word for wisdom and help? Do you know what the Bible says about your situation? Dig into God's Word and then live it out by faith!

God moves and we respond. God shows up and we act. That's the faith-rhythm of our life. The Word of God is filled with passages that

that echo Genesis 12. Abram, David, Mary, Daniel, Paul... Over and over we see a God-initiated encounter, leading to a God-made promise, leading to a faith-filled response by a 'normal' person. Just like us. Our lives are simplified when we don't hyperfocus on "God's part" or "my part." Instead, our great opportunity, every single day, is to follow the example of Abram in Genesis 12. We can get up and leave the place where we are, and head to the place where God is taking us—not knowing all the details, not knowing the exact path, and not necessarily knowing the plan or outcome. As we respond in obedience with a simple "yes," our faith is deepened as we trust the plan of God. Like the prophet Isaiah in his encounter with God in Isaiah 6, we can say daily, "Lord, here am I, send me!" This type of openness to God will take us places we never dreamed, and God will be there leading us on.

4. We Worship God

Worship is our response to God and His work in our lives. Worship is more than singing songs. Worship is a relationship built on trusting God, and it helps us surrender to God and His plan. When Abram heard God's promise, built an altar, and worshiped, it wasn't just an isolated incident. It was something he did throughout his life, as did others in the Old Testament. It was part of Abram's relationship with God.

Worship can look like trusting God about one big future promise—even when it seems out of reach. Worship can also look like stepping out in faith in small, daily opportunities. We may be called to move to a new city or change jobs. We may be given a task too big for us to accomplish in our own strength. We may see our children struggle, our parents struggle, our closest friends struggle. All of these moments give us a chance to trust God. Trust in God deepens our faith in God, knowing that what God promised will happen, guaranteed.

Every day, we have the chance to trust God with our past, present, and future. Worship flows from our lives each time we surrender to God's plan. This makes worship an active part of our life which is more than only going to church and singing songs. Worship is taking that step of faith, or responding to that nudge of the Holy Spirit. And in the hardest seasons, there are some core truths we can come back to so we can cultivate a heart of worship. We need to know—and believe—these truths so that worship is part of our daily journey.

God loves us, and He has a plan for our lives! Let that truth sink in. God loves you! He sees you! You are safe with God! To top it off, God has a plan for you! According to Romans 12:2, it's a good, pleasing, and perfect plan. Like Abram, our story is made up of more than what we can see or know from our limited perspective. God is with us, and He is for us. God is at work. He is on the move. We are making spiritual progress. Worship happens when we trust God for the seen and unseen plans knowing that He is directing every detail of our life.

God equips us through His Word! God's Word is filled with precepts for us to follow and promises for us to claim. Instead of navigating life based on our emotions or perspectives, we can navigate life based on the truth found in the Bible. Worship happens when we move beyond what we see or feel and follow God's truth. Knowing God's Word helps us place our trust in who God is, and how God faithfully works. And when we trust God, there is a peace that passes all understanding, that guards our hearts and our minds in Christ Jesus (Philippians 4:6-7).

This season provides the perfect opportunity to live by faith. Putting our eyes on Jesus helps us to trust God and follow him step-by-step. Instead of trying to manipulate or control the circumstances of life, we can march through life by faith. Our lives can proclaim that God is real, He has a plan for us, and we can trust Him no matter what. Worship happens each time we trust, believe, and surrender to God's way over our way. There's a sense of joy and satisfaction that we can't achieve through the world's methods or metrics. We can go through life with a full bank account, the biggest houses, and the coolest experiences…and still feel empty inside. Or, we can go through life with a sense of contentment because we trust God to take care of us and work through us in ways we never dreamed possible. In Philippians 4:11-13, the Apostle Paul talks about being content whether having everything or nothing.

God made some amazing (and unexpected) promises to Abram.… But, He made promises to us too! Like Abram, we may deal with overwhelming circumstances and big choices. But, like Abram, we have a certain future. Some day, we'll go to Heaven, of course. But in the here and now, what can we stake our claim on? What's something we can hold on to that is more than just 'pie in the sky' promises? What helps us in our actual lives? God doesn't promise magical fixes, but He promises that we can trust him. He promises that, in life and death, we are a child of God. Especially in the face of uncertain futures and big-time promises! We have the chance—every single day—to know and live for God, and to experience His promises in ALL of life.

As our journey continues, we're going to explore and define trust. We're going to process it together. Through the story of Abram, God shows us over and over that we can trust Him with the details, knowing He is on the move and all of it is according to His plan.

As believers in Jesus, we often forget that God's plan didn't start with the Gospels and New Testament. It started long before that, at the beginning, with Genesis. God was directing every detail, putting together every piece of the puzzle. When Jesus came, it was no accident that He was born into a certain family with a certain lineage.

In Abram, we see a person following God, and an invitation for us to do the same. Wherever we are in our faith walks, whether we're starting our journey with God or just starting our day, we can trust God. Do you need a fresh start or a fresh move of God in and through your life? Will you let go of anxiety, worry, and control? So the question for you is: God, can I trust you?

Transforming Truth:
Trust is Rooted in God.

"Oh Lord, we praise You: the One who sees, knows, cares, guides, and provides for us. You are personal and intimate with us. You are the One who has a specific plan for us, our loved ones, and our time here on this earth. Every single detail of our life is safe with You. There's not one thing that we face today that surprises You, that is too difficult for You, or that cannot be used for Your glory and for our good.

So, Lord, I pray that as we dig deep into the life of Abram that You would build faith in us. Thank You for the Bible, and help us to apply the truths to our lives. Lord, give us eyes to see, ears to hear, and hearts to know how You're moving.

Oh, Lord, we want to trust You. We want to know You. We want to love You. We want to serve You. May we be "all in" when it comes to You! It's in the powerful name of Jesus we pray, amen."

DISCUSSION QUESTIONS

As we journey through the life of Abraham, think about your life. What is God cultivating in you? How can faith and trust grow in your life? What is your greatest struggle? What is defining you in this season of your journey?

Chapter 1: God, Can I Trust You?

1. When you think of Abram (or Abraham) what parts of his story are familiar to you?
2. Share about a time when God showed up in your life and called you to take a step of faith. Maybe this was your salvation experience or an unexpected chance to follow God's plan.
3. God's Word is filled with promises for our day. How does God's Word shape you? Do you have a verse or passage of Scripture that is meaningful to you? Why is this passage meaningful in your journey with God?
4. What does obedience look like for you in this season of your journey? What is the next step of faith you need to take?

Often we look to people, things, or experiences to build our trust in God. This is a slippery slope because when things go wrong, our trust is shaken. Here's the deal: Trust begins with God!

- Trust is **not** dependent upon circumstances or the outcome of our circumstances.
- Trust is **not** dependent on ourselves or our resources.
- Trust is **not** about being in control or staying in control.
- **Trust is built on God.** He is our firm foundation!

This leads us to our Transforming Truth: Trust is Rooted in God!

5. Is trusting God hard for you? What are some of the barriers you face when it comes to trusting God and following His plan for your life?

CHAPTER 2

Hard Times Lead to a Choice

Abram faced trouble and hardship even while living in the place of promise. After the God-sized moment of Genesis 12:1-9, trouble was looming in Abram's future. Just because Abram was in Canaan, that didn't shield him from the challenges of real life. We don't know what was going through Abram's mind when he faced this challenge. Did he question, doubt, get frustrated, or go into problem-solving mode? What we do know is that the Bible does not skip over the challenging parts of the story. I love that! God wants you and me to be able to navigate our hard times. So, we have stories like Abram's recorded in the Bible.

As we dig into this part of the story, let's not judge Abram. Instead, let's learn from him. It's easy to examine certain Bible passages as though they're fictional case studies. Along the way, we may think or say, "I would never do that!" or "What was he thinking?" But, the moment we take that approach, we forget that the people in the Bible were real people trying to live out their faith in real-time. Like us, they had the chance to trust God and walk by faith. Like us, they also had the chance to mess up, sin, and hurt others.

For us, having a tender heart towards the people in the Bible helps us deepen our walk with God because we learn from them and their stories, instead of judging them for what they did or did not do. So, instead of judging Abram, we can try and ask some questions. "Why did Abram ask Sarai to lie about their marriage?" "How were women viewed in their culture?" "What might I have done to save my family?" And, most importantly, "How do lies impact my own walk with God?" Let's pick up the story and see how Abram dealt with a hard time in his life.

His Journey

To understand the next part of Abram's story, we have to realize that Abram and his family lived a semi-nomadic lifestyle, moving around to wherever they found food and water for themselves and their livestock. Whenever they used all of the food and water in a particular area, they would pick up their tents and move to a different place in the land.[13]

God had led Abram and his family to Canaan, the place of promise. Maybe they were full of hope and excitement for what God had next for them. God had promised land to them, and it was good land!

But then we read in Genesis 12 that a famine happened in the land, and everything changed. As we read about Abram's reaction to a hard time, we'll discover four key points, which will lead us to our transforming truth: *Hard times lead to a choice—do I trust God or myself?*

1. Trouble Happened to Abram

There was a famine in the land, so Abram went down to Egypt to stay there for a while because the famine in the land was severe.
Genesis 12:10

In some parts of the Bible we see that a famine was a specific consequence for sin; other times it was just noted as a time when the rain didn't fall and the ground didn't produce food. Whatever the reason, we always see that it had an impact on the people.

In fact, that was one reason God allowed famines to happen, so people would realize their need for Him. Famine led God's people to repent from their sins and turn from their stubborn independence from God. Over and over again, God used famine as a path to a deeper, more meaningful relationship with His people. This was exactly what was going on with Abram. What happened in Genesis 12:10 showed God's consistent work among His people, as He invited Abram to trust Him through a hard time.

Famines are hard no matter if they are minor or severe. We are not sure if this famine was a result of sin or simply a dry season that led to a hard time. One thing we do know is the famine revealed what was going on in Abram's heart. The tug of war between faith and fear was real.

Since the famine was severe the logical option for Abram and his family was to leave Canaan and go to a place that had food. This meant leaving the place of promise and heading to Egypt. I bet this was not an easy decision to make. Abram may have had some sleepless nights as he debated whether he and his family should leave Canaan.

Based on what happened in the rest of the story, I would suggest that Abram was struggling to trust God during this season of famine. Was Abram ready to lean on God during hard times? Or was he ready to lean on his own human logic?

2. Trouble Exposed Abram

When he was about to enter Egypt, he said to his wife Sarai, "Look, I know what a beautiful woman you are. When the Egyptians see you, they will

> say, 'This is his wife.' They will kill me but let you live. Please say you're my sister so it will go well for me because of you, and my life will be spared on your account."
> Genesis 12:11-13

Abram turned to Sarai as they entered Egypt and asked her to lie about their marriage. Why? There were probably a lot of reasons. Sarai was beautiful. In that day, women were often seen as property, not valued as individuals. Would Egyptians treat foreigners like Abram fairly? What if someone more powerful killed Abram and kidnapped Sarai? Would they be treated worse as a married couple than as 'siblings'? Trouble exposes either a *fear-filled heart* or a *faith-filled heart*. A fear-filled heart can lead to sin. A faith-filled heart can lead to stepping forward with God. Abram's request to Sarai came from a place of fear. The request was a symptom of a deeper problem.

Abram was having a hard time remembering God's promise to him about his own family. The promise was that Abram and Sarai would give birth to a child and the child would lead to a nation.Through that nation, the Messiah would come. God would not leave Sarai in Egypt as a wife of the Pharaoh and Abram lying dead in a ditch before they even had a child! As they crossed that border (and afterwards) Abram had a chance to confess his fear and to trust in God. He could have seen his fear-filled heart turn into a faith-filled heart. He could have focused on God's promises and instructions even if trouble showed up.

Instead, Abram took matters into his own hands, and the fear that was on the inside made its way to the outside. He didn't take his thoughts captive; he didn't align his feelings with the truth. He didn't remember who God was and how God was working in his life.

The trouble in Abram's life produced and revealed sin, but thankfully God was in control. God was fighting for Abram, and working in miraculous ways.

3. Sin Impacted Abram

> *When Abram entered Egypt, the Egyptians saw that the woman was a very beautiful woman. Pharaoh's officials saw her and praised her to Pharaoh, so the woman was taken to Pharaoh's household. He treated Abram well because of her, and Abram acquired flocks and herds, male and female donkeys, male and female slaves, and camels. But the Lord struck Pharaoh and his household with severe plagues because of Abram's wife, Sarai. Genesis 12:14-17*

Sin. It's real, and its impact is real. The moment Adam and Eve ate the forbidden fruit, sin entered the world and trouble became a reality everyone had to face. Because of sin, we live in a fallen world. Throughout the Bible, from Genesis to Revelation, we see people facing the consequences for their sins and the sins of others. In every circumstance, though, God was working.[14]

Sin always has consequences. What is a consequence? Basically, it is something that happens as a result or an effect of an action or condition.[15] When Abram lied about his relationship with Sarai, God responded with a plague that affected Pharaoh and his household. Something we see clearly in Abram's story is that consequences do not stay contained. When sin happened the consequences touched other people. Abram's trip to Egypt was the first time we see this in his life, but it will not be the last.

While the plague served as a teaching moment for Abram, it also displayed God's commitment to Abram. Through the plague, we can see God's plan to get Abram and his family back on the right path. But the consequences were going to be real for Abram and Sarai, as well as for the people around them; hurt for the people in Pharaoh's household, probably shame and guilt on Abram and Sarai's side. Maybe rumors and hatred from others affected by the plague? The 'little white lie' could have led to even more danger for Abram and Sarai.

4. God Protected Abram from himself

So Pharaoh sent for Abram and said, "What have you done to me?" Why didn't you tell me she was your wife? Why did you say, 'She's my sister,' so that I took her as my wife? Now here is your wife. Take her and go!" Then Pharaoh gave his men orders about him, and they sent him away with his wife and all he had."
Genesis 12:18-20

Is anyone else breathing a deep sigh of relief? Abram could have been killed; the Egyptians could have chased him out of Egypt or demanded all his possessions because of the lie Abram told Pharaoh. God protected Abram from Pharaoh, but God also protected Abram from Abram.

God showed up and was faithful to the promise even as Abram struggled to believe in the faithfulness of God. This is a theme we will see repeated in Abram's life.

As we read this passage, we need to remember it was happening against the backdrop of God's promise to Abram. God said He would make Abram into a great nation with many descendants. Even as Abram was struggling to navigate the fear in his heart, God was protecting

Abram's and Sarai's lives. I am thankful that God protects us from us! (I bet Abram would say the same thing.)

Even though Abram was not navigating well, he didn't go home destitute. Abram's time in Egypt made its mark on his family, as well as on others. It's easy to say that Abram shouldn't have left Canaan or that he shouldn't have lied about Sarai. Again, let's not judge; let's learn. Honestly, we might have done the same thing. The deeper question or issue is this: *What if Abram had trusted God no matter where he lived?*

What if Abram knew God would show up to protect and provide in Canaan or in Egypt? While Abram did not get it right this time, a day was coming when he would get it right. That day would require Abram to walk up the mountain with the most precious treasure ever given by God. I just wonder if the way God protected Abram and his family in Egypt helped shape Abram for the ultimate test of his faith in God?

Our Journey

One night, I was driving to an event to teach on the topic of trusting God. What most people didn't know was that I knew I was holding back from God and trying to stay in control of my life. I was scared underneath, and running out of energy to be 'the good girl.' On the outside everything looked great, but I was at the point of burnout and knew something had to change. I remember praying one of those flare prayers, "God if You get me through tonight, I will get serious about this control issue." God did get me through that night, and the next day I plunged into learning about trust.

-Andrea

Hard times find us one way or another. Either we sin and that leads to trouble or the impact of living in a fallen world leads to trouble. Here is the bottom line. We can't avoid trouble! Jesus made this clear before He went to the cross: "In this world you will have trouble..." (John 16:33). So, what are we going to do with the hard times we face? I am glad we can learn a few lessons from Abram and Sarai and their trip to Egypt.

1. Trouble Happens to Us

In our day we will experience famine, though not always literally. Most of us get our food from grocery stores, not livestock, but none of us can escape trouble or hard times. The doctor gives a hopeless diagnosis. A son or daughter is trapped in an unhealthy relationship. The supervisor says jobs are being cut. A misunderstanding between friends leads to heartbreak and alienation.

Hard times give us a chance to cultivate a faith-filled heart. But, having a faith-filled heart is not easy or automatic. Sometimes it's hard to remember that God is faithful to His promises, especially when trouble happens.

In life, there are ups and downs. There are twists and turns. Sometimes we are soaring high and other times, we're afraid we're going to crash into the ground. There's an easy trap we can fall into, of thinking, "When life is good, God is good, and I'm doin' good!" But what happens when life is NOT good? We'll be tempted to believe the opposite. "Life isn't good... I'm definitely not doin' good! Is God even good?" When trouble comes, it's easy to start doubting if God actually cares for us. It's easy to start wondering, "How have I messed up?" and slip into a works-based faith, thinking if we just do more things for God, He'll do something good for us. Or that if we did all those things, and He didn't do anything in return, we should walk away from Him. "This is happening, so I guess I can't trust God to watch my back." Stories like Abram's challenge us to take a step back and say, "God, I know you're good, and you're going to get me through. You're not the enemy in this situation. You're my refuge."

We can't let circumstances shape our idea of how God works. If our security depends on our circumstances, it leads to a fear-filled heart. We can obsess about what is going wrong, and what could go wrong next. We can resolve to 'just try harder' and do more good things.

In contrast, if our security depends on God, it leads to a faith-filled heart. We'll think about what Jesus already did for us on the cross. We'll remember that we are more than conquerors in Christ Jesus, and that God is with us and has a plan even in the hard moments.

Jesus is with us and life impacts us. Both are true. The next step—a hard step—is to surrender instead of panic. We engage in the situation doing what honors God, not acting from a fear-filled heart. We need practical steps to go along with our theological beliefs. Through Abram's story, we're coming face-to-face with this concept of trust during hard times. What was driving Abram as he entered Egypt was an internal dialogue. The same thing happens in our lives, with our thoughts. A practical step we can take to see where we are on our spiritual journey is asking the question, "What comes out of me during hard times?" Faith or Fear. The answer to that question empowers us to know our tendencies, and what or whom we're trusting. This gives us the pathway to walk for transformation.

2. Trouble Exposes Us

Whenever we don't know up from down, right from left, top from bottom...whatever is going on inside of us will eventually come out. A fear-filled heart focuses on worries, self-preservation, and selfish desires. A fear-filled heart tries to protect itself at any cost. Even lying or stretching the truth may seem OK. Hard times bring up whatever is buried deep inside. It might be a fear or an insecurity. It might be a sinful tendency or a blindspot. Once that fear-filled tendency surfaces it is only a matter of time before it is acted on or revealed.

We can learn from Abram and approach our famines differently. We can run toward God and His promises instead of running away from God. What is our perspective of the situation, and what is God's perspective? What are the incorrect thoughts about God, ourselves, and life that are drawing us to the fear-filled mindset? Maybe it's something about our circumstances that keeps us in a defeated mindset. Can we see how our circumstances are making a way for us to draw closer to God, instead of pushing Him further away?

Throughout Abram's journey, we'll study some of the lies he believed. Keep an eye out for those! Besides helping us understand him better, it'll help us understand ourselves better. Whatever lie Abram believed at the beginning, did he believe it at the end? When he took Isaac up that mountain, was that lie holding him back or had he left that lie behind? And if he left it behind, can we leave ours behind, too?

Identifying lies that come from the enemy or from ourselves about our circumstances help us expose what is driving us during trouble. We may have to do some digging, praying, journaling, and talking to friends who really know us to figure out the sinful patterns in our lives. What are the lies that we are believing that are contrary to God and His word? This is an important question that will help us expose sin and replace it with truth!

Then we don't stop with identifying the lies! We take the next step and *replace the lies with truth from the Scripture so that God's words are running through our heads instead of our own.* That, my friend, gives us the victory of a renewed mind in Jesus. When we renew our minds, we face life fortified with truth and faith. Then, when troubles pressure us, what comes out of us is not fear and sin. Instead, we produce the fruit of the Spirit: love, joy, peace, patience, kindness, goodness, faithfulness, gentleness, and self-control (Galatians 5:22-23).

3. Sin Impacts Us

Ultimately, in our faith journey, we will have moments where we're forced to confront the belief system we have in place. There will be an intersection—maybe even a crash—between a challenging circumstance and our beliefs. We will have to look at what we believe about God, ourselves, life, and others. What do we actually believe about God's goodness? What do we believe about our role in life? About our interactions with others? That provides the open door to renew our minds as we let go of the lies of the enemy and the lies that we've told ourselves. It's a door to the truth that is revealed in God's word.

Let's talk about the lies of the flesh. We live in a fallen and sinful world. Every single person is sinful. Scripture says, "For all have sinned and fall short of the glory of God" (Romans 3:23). Our sin nature (flesh) is drawn to the temporary things of this world like control, power, or possessions. Like Abram, we may try to protect ourselves or manipulate our circumstances. The way we go about it leads to sin during the process. So we bring all of that with us in this thing called life. If we don't have a spiritual game plan for renewing our minds, we are defeated before we get out of bed in the morning!

Let's talk about the lies of the enemy. We have a very real enemy: Satan. Once a prideful angel, cast out of heaven, he still fights against God and against us. His intention in our lives is to steal, kill, and destroy (John 10:10). One of the main ways he does that is by trying to trick us into believing his lies so we turn away from God. Satan tries to distract us, harm us, and control us. Thankfully God is greater than Satan, and God makes us greater than the pull of sin and self. Satan does have some power over this world, but it's under God's authority. As you're living your life you'll be tempted to believe his lies—all humans are. His lies intend to lead you to places of fear, frustration, hopelessness, and ultimately death. Our sinful nature is drawn to Satan's lies, and in our own way we rebel against God and the truth taught in the Bible.

God wants us to be aware of who Satan is and how he works so we can meet his lies with truth and faith. And God wants us to be aware of our own sinful nature so that we can combat those lies the same way.

For example, a lie of the enemy might be: "You're unlovable. Your life has no purpose or meaning. God could never use someone like you." The lie from our sinful nature might be: "You'll only be loved if you're beautiful or needed. Your life will only have a purpose if you give 110% all the time. God can only use you if you're successful." But what is God's truth? In answer to those lies, He says, "You are unconditionally loved by Me. I have a purpose for you. And I will use you in amazing ways, no matter how you feel or the circumstances you face!" Take a look at the **Lies vs. Truth** chart and see if you fall into the trap of believing a lie. If so, replace it with God's truth!

LIES VS. TRUTH [16]

L • God doesn't love me.
T • God loves me and cares for me. (1 Peter 5:7)

L • I'm not good enough or perfect enough the way I am.
T • I am fearfully and wonderfullly made just the way I am. (Psalm 139:13-14)

L • God should fix my problems.
T • Everyone struggles but I can be encouraged because Jesus has already won the battle. (John 16:33)

L • I'm not worth anything.
T • I get to choose who controls my life. (Romans 6:13)

L • I can't help the way I am.
T • I get to choose who controls my life. (Romans 6:13)

L • I can sin and get away with it.
T • My sin entangles me and keeps me from living in victory. (Hebrews 12:1-2)

L • My sin isn't really that bad. Isn't hurting anyone else.
T • Sin matters because it shows who I'm in relationship with or not. (1 John 5:18)

L • God can't forgive what I have done.
T • If I confess and repent, He forgives me. (John 1:9)

L • I can't walk in consistent victory over sin.
T • I can walk worthy of Jesus through His power. (Colossians 1:10)

L • I can make it without consistent time in the Word and prayer.
T • When I seek Him first, He takes care of all the other things. (Matthew 6:3)

L • I have to have a husband to be happy.
T • God has good plans for me, and His timing is perfect. I can trust Him. (Jeremiah 29:11)

L • It is my responsibility to change my mate.
T • I need to be a godly woman and trust God to be the Holy Spirit. (Proverbs 31:10-12)

L • If I feel something, it must be true.
T • My heart can be deceitful. I need to test everything against Scripture. (Jeremiah 17:9)

L • I shouldn't have to suffer.
T • Suffering develops holiness in me. (Romans 5:3-5)

L • I will only be happy or feel valuable if my career is successful.
T • My value and worth come from being a child of the King. (Deuteronomy 7:6)

L • I will always be sad and depressed.
T • He can heal my pain and give me joy. (Isaiah 61:1-3)

L • I am damaged goods. No one will ever want me.
T • He loves me with an everlasting love. (Jeremiah 31:3-4)

L • I'm useless and can't do anything right.
T • He is my strength and I can do anything God calls me to do. (Philippians 4:13)

L • I am trapped in fear.
T • God is with me and fear has no hold on me. (Psalm 23:4)

L • I'm alone. No one really cares about me.
T • I am treasured (1 Peter 2:9) and the Lord is ALWAYS with me. (Deuteronomy 31:8)

What starts with a whisper from the enemy can be fed by the things around us, like advertisements and peer pressure. Until we notice the lies and fight them with God's truth, they'll just root deeper in our lives. The question here is: *Whose voice will we believe?*

4. God Protects Us from Us

Trouble will happen. Trouble will produce and reveal something in us—either faith or fear. We can build in protection so fear is exposed and faith is expressed, while also trusting that God can and will protect us from ourselves when we mess up.

We saw how God had a plan even while Abram and Sarai were trying to save their own skins by lying. It may be uncomfortable to read, but what can we learn from this part of the story? *God is faithful to the promise He makes even when we are not.* God is faithful to the word He gave us, even when we question if things will work out. God is working in the big picture to position us for victory even when we are sabotaging ourselves! Not only that, God is faithful to the promise when the people around us don't know about the promise! God in His sovereignty, providence, and plan is always at work. He is blessing and frustrating. He's reorganizing and positioning. Through it all, God reveals our fear-filled hearts. He does that on purpose, wanting to lead His people to repent and have a faith-filled heart instead.

This does not mean God will save His people from wrong or mistaken choices, or from consequences. Even though God has a plan for our long-term good, the consequences of sin are real. We think of consequences as bad or harsh and sometimes they are. But sometimes they are good consequences, or at least the road to good things. In Abram's story, the consequences did at least two things. One, they showed him that his actions affected others besides himself. Two, they reminded Abram that he could trust God even when life was uncertain.

What about us? We don't have to wonder if taking the path of fear and sin will have long-term consequences. We know it will. If we want to escape the trap of sin, we have to ask God to protect us. It also helps to build accountability into our lives so that there are guardrails along the way to help us pause and reset. A guardrail could be an accountability partner who we share our struggles with. It could be a Scripture passage that's a lifeline when we feel a familiar temptation creeping up in us. Maybe it's journaling so we can get out on paper what is actually going on inside of us. We need renewing rhythms in our life so we can identify the fear, confess any sin, and move forward in faith.

Our ultimate protection comes through Jesus. God extended a promise through Jesus Christ and He secured our eternal future in heaven in glory with God forever. While we will have trouble, we have a protected future because this world is not our home. We will go home to be with God in glory. We will be free of sin, we will be free of death, we will be free of disease and tears and hardships and trials and famine and overwhelming circumstances! God will wipe away every tear from our eyes (Revelation 21:4), and we will worship the Lord in spirit and truth (John 4:23) around the throne, with every tongue, tribe, people, and nation together (Revelation 7:9). But we're not there yet.

Like Abram, we have to face hard seasons and make choices in real-time. Am I going to trust God? Will I draw near to God by walking the path of faith? Or am I going to trust myself by trying to survive on my own? All of us could probably share stories about the paths we've taken—good and bad—over the years! Thankfully, God is going before us and coming behind us every step of the way. He protects us from the enemy and from ourselves. God has a plan and we can trust him.

Transforming Truth:
Hard Times Lead to a Choice - Do I Trust God or Myself?

"Lord, we thank You for who You are, and for how You're so faithful to work in and through us for Your glory. Even during difficulties and questioning, we choose individually and together to press into You. We choose to run hard after You instead of running away from You. We choose to build renewing rhythms into our life so that we are less likely to get off track and more likely to follow Your plan. And even as we choose to do all these things, we thank You that You first chose us. You are leading us, and making a way for us. Lord, help us when we are in seasons of trouble. Help us to see Your presence and provision even if it comes in unexpected ways. Thank You that hard times lead to a choice. May we always choose Your way over ours. It is in the powerful name of Jesus we pray, amen."

DISCUSSION QUESTIONS

As we journey through the life of Abraham, think about your life. What is God cultivating in you? How can faith and trust grow in your life? What is your greatest struggle? What is defining you in this season of your journey?

Chapter 2: Hard Times Lead to a Choice!

1. During hard times, do you question, doubt, get frustrated, or go into problem-solving mode? What do these types of responses reveal about your trust in God? (This is a safe place for you to be real!)
2. A few of the questions I ask during hard times include, "Lord, what's going on down here? Lord, do you see me? Lord, do you care? Lord, do you have a plan for me in the middle of this?" And, my all-time favorite, "Lord, why does life have to be so hard?!" What questions do you ask God during hard times?
3. In your own words, describe the difference between a fear-filled heart and a faith-filled heart. Share an example of a fear-filled heart or a faith-filled heart from your own life.
4. Lies of the enemy and lies of the flesh are real! All of us believe things that are not based on God's Word. During our study of Abraham, we will see how lies impacted Abraham's ability to trust God, especially during hard times. Why is it important to base our lives on God's truth? How do you recognize lies in your life and replace the lies with the truth found in God's Word? Share a lie of the flesh or lie of the enemy that you struggle with on a regular basis.

All of us know what it is like to face a hard time. For many years when a hard time hit, I immediately jumped to the worst-case scenario and asked all the questions. To be honest, I still ask lots of questions and get rattled more than I like to admit! But, I have learned something very helpful in my walk with God. When a hard time hits, I watch my actions and reactions and then trace them back to either a right or wrong belief about God. Talk about renewing on steroids! That is what a hard time offers us: an opportunity to renew our minds as we trust God.

This leads to our Transforming Truth: Hard times lead to a choice - do I trust God or myself?

5. Can you embrace your hard times as an opportunity to trust God and renew your mind? If so, how can you do this?

CHAPTER 3

Trusting God Leads to Intimacy with God

Abram blew it when he was in Egypt. He told Pharaoh that Sarai was his sister instead of his wife, and that led to consequences for everyone. But I believe he came out of Egypt with a new perspective of God and a new perspective of himself. He went back to Canaan, the land of promise, and settled in a new place—a place where he could meet with God.

It encourages me to know that Abram's trip to Egypt didn't define him and that our "trips" don't have to define us. Hard times don't have to determine our character or the trajectory of our lives. We feel the worry and the struggles, but the trouble-filled season is not the end of our story. We can come out on the other side transformed instead of hanging our heads. Instead of having a fear-filled heart, we can have a faith-filled heart. And having a faith-filled heart leads to intimacy with God.

His Journey

Abram returned to Canaan, and God was about to move powerfully. Not only was God going to remind Abram of the promise but he was also going to deepen the reality of the promise. Along the way, Abram was going to learn how to come out of a hard season and be transformed by God.

Let's jump into Genesis chapter thirteen, and discover four key points, which will lead us to our transforming truth: *Trusting God leads to intimacy with God.*

1. Abram Went Back to the Place of Worship

Abram went up from Egypt to the Negev—he, his wife, and all he had, and Lot with him. Abram was very rich in livestock, silver, and gold. He went by stages from the Negev to Bethel, to the place between Bethel and Ai where his tent had formerly been, to the site where he had built an altar. And Abram called on the name of the Lord from there.

Genesis 13:1-4

I bet it was quite the scene as Abram and his family made their journey from Egypt back to Canaan. I wonder what the Canaanites thought when he traveled back with all those animals and riches, like a rancher who had increased his herds and was moving to a new ranch.

What we don't want to miss was the focus of Abram to go back to the place of worship. Scripture says that Abram went back to where he had last built an altar, near Bethel. If you remember, back in Genesis 12, Abram was near Bethel when God made the initial promise of many descendants and land for those descendants. In response to that encounter, Abram built an altar and worshiped God there.

Abram had time for regrouping and thinking about life after leaving Egypt, and he could have settled anywhere in the land. I think it's fascinating that he went back to Bethel, back to the place where he and God had had such a special meeting before. From there, he could move on with what God had for him, to the next season of life. So, what did Abram do? He called on the name of the Lord at Bethel. What did it mean to 'call on the name of the Lord?' Was it a time of quiet reflection? Singing? Proclaiming God's name aloud? We don't know exactly. We just know that moment was important to him, so he marked it in his life with worship.

At the heart of worship is an understanding that God is God. He knows what is best, and He is faithful to lead. Spending time with God provided the right perspective for Abram. He had been through a hard season in Egypt (due to his and Sarai's choice to deceive Pharaoh), but instead of hiding somewhere in shame, he turned his heart back to God.

2. Abram Pursued Peace

It's a good thing that Abram had taken the time to call on the Name of the Lord because there was plenty of trouble waiting for him in Canaan. Abram needed the Lord's wisdom to lead his growing household and all their livestock.

> *Now Lot, who was traveling with Abram, also had flocks and herds and tents. But the land was unable to support them as long as they stayed together, for they had so many possessions that they could not stay together, and there was quarreling between the herdsmen of Abram's livestock and the herdsmen of Lot's livestock. (At that time the Canaanites and Perizzites were living in the land.)*
> *Genesis 13:5-7*

Remember, Abram (and Lot) had gotten richer in Egypt. More animals, more people, more tents and things. Abram's and Lot's herdsmen started arguing, which brought more tension into Abram's life.

Let's look at one small sentence at the end of this section. "The Canaanites and Perizzites were also living in the land." The fact that the Canaanites and the Perizzites saw the arguments among Abram's family should be a red flag to us. God was raising Abram up to be the father of a nation and to create a lineage for the Messiah. One of God's purposes was to show that He had claimed a nation for His own, and to show the difference between that nation and others. To show the difference it makes when living to God, with God, for God and through God. To contrast the One True God with the 'little g' gods that never really changed anyone's life.

Arguing and fighting did not line up with God's plan for His special people and their witness in the land. God knew He was going to make Abram and his descendants into a nation that was different because they worshiped the One True God, but there may not have been much of a visible difference at that point.

So Abram said to Lot, "Please, let's not have quarreling between you and me, or between your herdsmen and my herdsmen, since we are relatives. Isn't the whole land before you? Separate from me: if you go to the left, I will go to the right; if you go to the right, I will go to the left."
Genesis 13:8-9

Was this cultural negotiation or unusual humility? Did Abram have to defer to Lot or did Lot have to defer to Abram? I'm not sure. One thing we can know is that Abram knew it wasn't sustainable for him and Lot to stay together. The land couldn't take care of both. A choice had to be made. Hopefully, the choice would lead to peace in the family.

3. Abram Trusted God

Abram opened the door for Lot to pick the place where he wanted to live. Could Abram trust Lot to act in Abram's best interests? Probably not. Could Abram lie and scheme and bully his way into more riches or the right location for himself? Probably so. Did Abram do any of that? Absolutely not. Instead, he left the choice up to Lot. Maybe Abram really didn't care, or maybe Abram just trusted God with whatever would happen. Or maybe both. We've talked about how our actions are different when we have a faith-filled heart instead of a fear-filled heart. I believe that this is a moment where we see Abram actively trusting God, boosted by that time of worship at Bethel.

Lot went to the plains of the Jordan and Abram went back into Canaan to the open land. The decisions of where to settle had massive implications for Lot and Abram. I think it's unlikely that Lot didn't know how the people in Sodom lived, but maybe Lot was tempted by the rich land and thought Sodom wouldn't influence him. Sometimes we don't think we'll fall into temptation, so we stay close to it instead of avoiding it. That area held incredible settled land, with lush pastures guaranteeing happy herds, and a place for his tents close to cities. (I wonder if his wife and daughters enjoyed city life?)

So Lot chose the entire plain of the Jordan for himself. Then Lot journeyed eastward, and they separated from each other. Abram lived in the land of Canaan, but Lot lived in the cities on the plain and set up his tent near Sodom. (Now the men of Sodom were evil, sinning immensely against the Lord.)
Genesis 13:11-13

Abram went back to the land of Canaan and he had an encounter with God. God reconfirmed the promise; God responded to the obedience and faith of Abram. By moving back to Canaan and away from Sodom and Gomorrah, Abram moved away from the distractions and drama of the people there, but also away from drama and distractions with Lot. By parting ways with Lot, Abram removed himself from conflict over land and property. For Abram, the less inviting place turned out to be the better place. It's such a picture of God's plan, which sometimes seems so upside-down. The things we think are lush and inviting fall short of providing what we need, while the more challenging places hold extra blessings for us!

4. God Reminded Abram of the Promise

After Lot left, God initiated another encounter with Abram.

After Lot had separated from him, the Lord said to Abram, "Look from the place where you are. Look north and south, east and west, for I will give you and your offspring forever all the land that you see. I will make your offspring like the dust of the earth, so that if anyone could count the dust of the earth, then your offspring could be counted. Get up and walk around the land, through its length and width, for I will give it to you."
Genesis 13:14-17

God was saying, "Check it out! Look how good I am! All of this is yours; there's no area of the land you won't get to experience. And, listen, those mistakes you made didn't ruin your future. You didn't lose the promise. Everything I promised to you and your descendants—walk around and see it!" Abram needed to know that his past did not define him. His present reality did not have to overwhelm him. His unknown future did not have to scare him.

Can you imagine Abram traveling around, open-mouthed, feeling God's faithfulness with every footstep? God always had a plan, and God was protecting that plan even when Abram wasn't. How deep. How rich.

> *So Abram moved his tent and went to live near the oaks of Mamre at Hebron, where he built an altar to the Lord.*
> *Genesis 13:18*

We don't know how long or far Abram traveled throughout Canaan, but his next stop was in Hebron, near the giant trees of Mamre. The name Mamre can be translated as "richness or strength"[17] and then the word Hebron can be translated as "communion,"[18] meaning intimate connection. You may have heard the word 'communion' used in the sense of the Lord's Supper, which is exactly what we do when we take the Lord's Supper. We take the time to be fully present with God and remember what Jesus did for us on the Cross. Abram communed with God in Mamre.

When I think of Mamre and Abram's time there, I picture the wind blowing through the huge oak trees and peaceful surroundings. Maybe Abram and his household sat around their campfires and shared stories. His servants and shepherds could have taken advantage of the pause in the journey to have babies, to grow their own families. Maybe the word got out that this rich, childless man walked with the One True God and was a good boss for herders looking for work and security. Maybe Abram slipped away to escape the noise for long walks with God, grateful for God's presence while waiting for his own promised baby.

As he lived in the land next to the trees, Abram had the opportunity for deep, intimate interaction with God. If he had stayed in the struggle with Lot, he might never have had this chance.

Our Journey

I asked Jesus into my heart when I was a little girl. I was six years old, but let me tell you, just because I was little doesn't mean I didn't have big, extraordinary faith! I believed in God! I loved God! There was nothing my God couldn't do. I knew God had saved me, and all my trust, all my faith, and all my hope was in Him. I was open and gave up control of my life (as much as a six-year-old could). I was expecting, I was excited, I was all in with God because I knew He was all in with me.

When I think about my favorite seasons with God, of pure worship, that six-year-old me is right up there with the best. But, I was much older when I finally understood what it meant to really trust God with the details of my life.

-Andrea

In Genesis 13, there are so many parts of Abram's story that are easy to relate to. Like him, we have seasons of starting over, trying to reorient our lives. We also have seasons where we're caught up in a conflict and have to get our bearings. Or just when we think we've figured out what's next, there are power struggles that make it feel like there's no space left for us to grow and thrive. But if there was hope for Abram, all those years ago, there's hope for us!

1. We Go Back to the Place of Worship

Let's be honest, we all have those times in life when we don't know what to do. Abram had them. I've had them. You've had them. You may be stuck in one now. You may think, "I know God is working. I know he's doing something, but I don't know what it is. And I'm not sure how to move forward from here." In moments like these, we need to go back to our Bethel! We do this by going back in our hearts to that last place where we know God spoke and moved. Remembering the depth of our level of trust in that moment, and trusting God to move us forward from there.

When we go back to the place of worship it reminds us of everything that we know about God; it reminds us of His faithful work in and through our lives. Then we have that strength we need to move forward in faith.

Abram went back to the place where he had worshiped before. Centuries later, Paul wrote to the church in Colossae, "So then, just as you received Christ Jesus as Lord, continue to walk in him..." (Colossians 2:6-7). When we look at that verse, it reminds us to go back to living just as we lived when we first received Jesus.

There are times when we're in a new season, choosing where to go. We may not be deciding where to find water and grass for our animals, but we need to find a new home for our family, a new job, or a place to find friends. In those transition times, going back to the place of worship is like going back to the basics. But more than that, it's looking for the things we loved before and the ways God spoke or moved before.

It's a reminder to us to go back in order to move forward. When we've lost our way, we go back to what we knew. The lessons we once learned help us to move on now. When we received Christ, when we started our faith journey, we surrendered to God's love, mercy, grace, and forgiveness. We understood the impact of sin and the beauty of surrender. We don't think about that often enough—we just want to move ahead. We tell each other, "Don't dwell on the past." But there's grounding that happens when we remember the times we've heard from the Lord—in a sermon, in the Bible, or driving down the road and remembering, "There is hope!" Remembering that God is God brings us to a place of worship.

So when you're coming out of a hard season and trying to get your bearings, go back to the place of worship. That place—physical or in our memories—reminds us who God is and who we are in relationship to God. It gives us that infusion of hope, that sense of purpose and drive. We have passion and a desire to follow him. That's what going back can do. It gives us our grounding or bearing so that we know how to move forward.

Let's go back to the place of worship, remember what we know about God, and start living with purpose.

2. We Pursue Peace

Most of us won't have land conflicts but we have our own share of conflict at work, at church, or—like Abram—with our own family. When I look at how Abram handled this dynamic, I see him being honest, loving, and resolved. He knew that when we trust God with the end result, it's easier for us to navigate conflict and power struggles.

Sometimes we avoid conflict to 'keep the peace.' There's a difference, though, between passively *keeping* peace and actively *pursuing* peace. In a situation where we need to seek peace, we're not responsible for other people. We're responsible for ourselves, for our attitudes, actions, and reactions. We ask God for what to say, so our words honor Him and bring deliberate healing instead of deliberate hurt. And we can ask Him for our words to lay the groundwork for redemption and reconciliation.

Situations where we can't fix things are hard. Those are moments we have to trust God. But we don't have to lie, or act like something is OK when it's not. Living in peace means seeking resolution by doing what God lays on your heart, and trusting Him with the outcome. This is why it is so important to talk to God before we respond. We need a word from the Word when life gets messy! Sometimes we may have the luxury of a week of prayer and preparation before an upcoming confrontation. Other times, in the heat of an argument, we can just grab thirty seconds to silently ask God for the right words and attitude.

Our human tendency is often to 'clean house' and tell others what we think has been done wrong. We may react with frustration or passive aggression as we try to quickly solve issues. But none of that is pursuing peace.

God's way of redemption is better. We may never have to divide land, but we can choose peace in our own conflicts. We don't deny the truth of a situation, but we rely on God to speak into a situation or to move as only He can move. Sometimes we have to get out of the way for that to happen, like Abram did. Other times we need to speak up or step up in a

Christlike way for what is right. We can choose to let others go first, to actively offer suggestions that benefit others instead of just ourselves.

Certainly, we always want to be ready to give an answer for the hope we have in Jesus, but we give the answer dripping with love, gentleness, respect, and grace (1 Peter 3:15). *We can live with a heart not to be right in a situation but to point people to the One who is right.*

We are God's chosen people as believers in Jesus Christ. In 1 Peter 2:9, it talks about how we are a royal priesthood, a holy nation of people belonging to God, and how we've been brought out of darkness and into his marvelous light. We live in a fallen world that is full of people who need to see the difference Jesus makes in us.

But what do people often see from those of us who say we follow Jesus? They see us quarreling with one another. Debates, arguments, and pressure to follow certain standards. It's like we think we have this obligation to prove what is right or who is wrong. They see us being negative on social media and in our faith communities, just being ugly to each other. Our testimony is on the line when conflict comes—and most of the time we don't even realize it!

Through all this, Jesus is our perfect model. Jesus came to seek, save, and serve. The Scriptures remind us to speak the truth in love, not to force the truth on others in self-righteousness. As we're living in this fallen world, we need to seek peace and pursue it. We need to give up the right of being right and live right instead. Instead of trying to do the convicting, we can leave that to Jesus. We can focus on our words, actions, and reactions trusting God every step of the way.

3. We Trust God with the Outcome

I love thinking about Abram sitting at the trees of Mamre soaking up the friendship of God. Knowing that God was teaching Abram, and Abram was focusing on God, makes me long for that trusting relationship in my life, too.[19] In Mark 9:24, we read about a man crying out to Jesus, "I do believe—help my unbelief!" Sometimes we do trust God—a little—but how can we learn to trust him more?

"Trust is an assured reliance on the character, the ability, the strength or truth of someone or something, and as a result a willingness exists to place our confidence in that person or thing." [20]

I remember the first time I read this definition of trust. It was a light bulb moment. I had been asking God, "How can I trust you? How can I build my trust in you?" Right there in the definition was the answer. If I wanted to trust God, I needed to know His character, ability, strength, and truth! We can remember this with the acronym CAST.

C - Character
A - Ability
S - Strength
T - Truth

God's Character + His Ability + His Strength + His Truth = Our confidence in God. A simple way to remember this is to know that when trouble hits, we CAST our lives and our situations at the feet of Jesus!

Let's think about each part of this definition and how it helps us to trust God.

- **CHARACTER:** First, His character is who God is. The Bible is filled with details about who God is. We remember that He is Jehovah Jireh, the God who provides (Genesis 22:14). He is El Roi, the God who sees (Genesis 16:14-15). One of my favorite verses about God is really simple. It says, "Know that the Lord is God. It is He who made us, and we are His, we are His people, the sheep of His pasture" (Psalm 100:3, NIV). When trouble hits, we can remember that God is our Shepherd and Creator. He is our loving Father who takes care of us, no matter the situation. When we understand the character of God, we line our troubles up against the truth found in the Bible. The truth protects our hearts and our minds as we remember who God is and keep our focus on Him.
- **ABILITY:** Second, His ability is what God can do. What can God do? Scripture says that nothing is impossible for Him (Luke 1:37). A familiar passage of Scripture is found in Matthew 5 and tells of God's ability and willingness to take care of His creation, especially the people He created in His image. When trouble hits, I need to remember the ability of God to move. His ability isn't limited to His power, but includes His deep sense of care and compassion as well. "Praise be to the Lord, to God our Savior, who daily bears our burdens" (Psalm 68:19, NIV). He is the loving father inviting His child to bring Him every problem because He is capable of carrying those burdens. Whenever we really understand what God can do in the midst of our overwhelming circumstances, faith and trust replace our fear and doubt.
- **STRENGTH:** Third, His strength is how He works. God is present, active, and providing in every situation we face. All of us know what

it's like to be out of strength and at the end of our rope. We feel ourweakness and long for God's strength. In every moment, God is onthe throne, He is going before us, and He is making the path straight. God's strength is seen in how He accomplishes tasks in our lives. Isaiah 25:1 gives insight into the strength of God with two keywords. "O Lord, you are my God; I will exalt you and praise your name, for in perfect faithfulness you have done marvelous things, things planned long ago" (NIV). How does God work? He works in perfect faithfulness. He is always at work, even taking what others meant for evil and turning it into good (Genesis 50:20). When trouble hits, I have to remember that God is working through the trouble and is faithful to bring purpose out of the pain and meaning out of the mess.

- **TRUTH:** Fourth, His truth is His pure intentions towards us. I want to camp here for a moment because we have to know this one! We need to know that God is love and that He has good intentions towards us (1 John 4:7-21). We also need to know that God is light and there's not a shadow of darkness in Him—not a shadow, friend (1 John 1:5)! God is with you. God is for you. God is fighting your battle. God is positioning you for victory. I love this point, and Abram's life echoes it. God is for you even when you are not for yourself! His intentions are pure because He is holy, set apart, and pure. "The Lord is faithful to all His promises and loving toward all He has made" (Psalm 145:13, NIV). That's the God you serve. When trouble hits, I need to remember that God is not out to get me but He is out to save me. And His ability to save is greater than any trouble I will ever face.

We can CAST our trouble on God because we trust Him rather than ourselves or our circumstances! When we know God's character, ability, strength, and truth, our confidence in Him grows. Isaiah 32:17 will become a reality in our life: "The fruit of righteousness will be peace, the effect of righteousness will be quietness and confidence forever" (NIV). This does not mean we will not have to work through the hard seasons; that will always be a part of our lives. But imagine what it would be like for you to walk through your hard season with a quiet confidence in Jesus. What difference would that make in your life?

4. God Reminds Us of the Promise

Abram made a choice to actively pursue peace, and moved on with his life, away from Lot. As much as we can worry before a decision, the doubts don't always disappear afterward. *Did I make the right choice? Was that a crazy faith step? Did I hear God's voice right?*

We also can choose the paths that look inviting and easy. We don't know how Abram felt in the aftermath of yet another move. But God showed up to reconnect with him and to remind him of the promise.

Maybe you are overwhelmed by life. God is at work right now to provide a path for you to trust him as you know His character, His ability, His strength, and His truth. When we put our confidence in circumstances, our lives become reactive—we react to events and people and situations around us. Contrast that with God—unshakably good, unchangeably loving. In the good and the bad, God is the same; He is with us and for us. That gives us strength to face our days.

I'm writing to the woman who wants to trust God but is literally terrified at the thought of it. I want you to know for many years I was that woman. I had a wrong belief about who God was and how God worked. Maybe I am describing you. Maybe you've had wrong beliefs about God's character, or His strength. Maybe it's something about God's ability or truth.

We may feel defined by hard seasons like sickness or money worries. When we let go of our own need to define and control situations, it can be life-changing. Life-giving. It frees us up to see everything else that He has for us, things we're blinded to as long as we cling to our human perspective. If we can reset our thinking, we can see that God is purposeful in all His ways. He's working all things together for good as we walk with Him. That's the big-picture relationship we can have with God. What He has for us is never exhausted; there's always more. We never get to the end with Him! In Galatians 5:1 we read, "For freedom, Christ set us free….." In John 10:10 we read about an overabundant life for us: "…life and have it in abundance." It's like the Old Testament version of Abram enjoying intimacy with God even when life was not perfect.

God is always stripping away, He's refocusing, He is reminding us what really matters and what really counts. The implication here for us is that the prize is not "Sodom" or "Canaan," it's a relationship with God. He is helping us to have a vision that is so much bigger than the temporary. Through that process, we have the chance for communion with God, intimately interacting with Him. We're going to experience the joy that comes from our relationship with God, not from our circumstances.

We're on a journey that is moving us toward glory. What we do here matters, but ultimately our home is with God for all eternity. In the meantime, life produces and reveals what's going on inside of us. In the midst of our hard circumstances, what would it look like for us to have intimacy with God?

Transforming Truth:
Trusting God Leads to Intimacy with God.

> "Lord, we thank you for Your Word. Thank you for this truth that can saturate our hearts and our minds and transform us into Your likeness. Each day we choose to remember Your character, ability, strength, and truth so that our confidence is in You, not ourselves. Please draw us into deep intimacy with you. Help us to push beyond control, and push beyond the superficial. We want to truly be open to You moving in our lives, for Your glory. In Jesus' name, amen."

DISCUSSION QUESTIONS

As we journey through the life of Abraham, think about your life. What is God cultivating in you? How can faith and trust grow in your life? What is your greatest struggle? What is defining you in this season of your journey?

Chapter 3: Trusting God Leads to Intimacy with God

1. Abram went back to the place of worship and remembered how God worked in his life. This step helped Abram know how to move forward. We can do the same thing! A great way to "go back to the place of worship" is by identifying the spiritual marker moments in our lives. One way to discover these moments is by creating a spiritual timeline, identifying the moments when God moved in our lives and we responded in faith. Create a spiritual timeline for your life and share it with others.
2. Abram trusted God with the tension between his people and Lot's people. How do family and friend dynamics impact your focus? Do you trust God when tension rises and power struggles form? How can we seek and pursue peace during tense moments?
3. We introduced an important definition of trust. This definition invites us to know the character, ability, strength, and truth of God so that our confidence is in God. Here is a quick recap:
   - **Character:** Who God is.
   - **Ability:** What God can do.
   - **Strength:** How God accomplishes tasks in our lives.
   - **Truth:** God's Pure Intentions Along the Way.

   How does this definition frame or reframe your concept of trust? Is there one area of the definition that is hard for you to accept? For example, do you struggle to believe that God has pure intentions toward you and your family? Or do you struggle to trust God because you don't really know His character?
4. **Confidence** in God is the result of trusting God. Do you have confidence in God's ability and willingness to work in and through your life? What steps can you take so your confidence in God grows stronger?

This leads to our Transforming Truth: Trusting God leads to Intimacy with God.

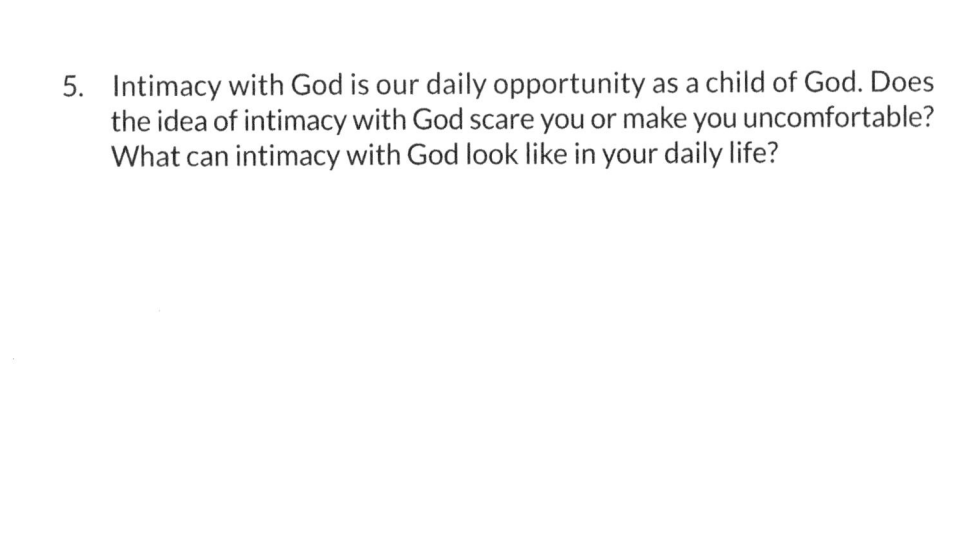

5. Intimacy with God is our daily opportunity as a child of God. Does the idea of intimacy with God scare you or make you uncomfortable? What can intimacy with God look like in your daily life?

Chapter 4

God-Sized Moments

Something that amazes me about God's story is how each part influences the last as the story unfolds. For example, Genesis 14 is going to mean more to us because we walked through Genesis 13. The beauty of God's Word is that it is one continuous story of God's love, mercy, grace, and relentless pursuit.

Remember where we left Abram and Lot? Abram had gone back to the trees of Mamre, which represented intimacy with God. But Lot had settled in the plains of Jordan close to Sodom, which led to some intense developments. *The places we go, the people we're with, and the things we do—they all impact our journey.* We're going to find in Genesis 14 two completely different situations that Abram and Lot found themselves in.

His Journey

After all their travels, Mamre must have seemed like a good resting place for Abram and his growing household. Even though they were nomads, a peaceful area with friendly neighbors would have been a good place to settle for a while and graze their herds. Then, suddenly, we read in Genesis 14 about a war starting in the area! It was the first recorded battle in Scripture and any time we see a 'first' in Scripture we want to pay close attention to it. The war started between several kings of different lands, who formed alliances and fought over possessions, people, boundaries, and land. (Some things never change!) One of the battles took place near Sodom and Gomorrah, right where Lot had chosen to settle. One day, a servant came and told Abram that Lot and his family had been captured. In the blink of an eye, a battle landed in Abram's lap. What would he do?

Let's jump into Genesis 14. We'll discover four key points, which will lead us to our transforming truth—*trusting God leads to God-sized moments*.

1. Abram's Preparation Led to Progress

One of the survivors came and told Abram the Hebrew, who lived near the Oaks belonging to Mamre the Amorite, the brother of Eshcol and the brother of Aner. They were bound by a treaty with Abram. When Abram heard that his relative had been taken prisoner, he assembled his 318 trained men, born in his household, and they went in pursuit as far as Dan.
Genesis 14:13-14

While Abram was living at the great trees of Mamre, he wasn't passively living. He built alliances with people in the region he could trust—Amorite neighbors. Abram created a community of people who were with him and for him. As a wealthy man with livestock and riches, he had a household that included hundreds of servants, shepherds, and workers. Among those were 318 trained men—his own private army. Even while Abram was enjoying intimacy with God in a season of rest, he was also preparing for seasons ahead of him.

Preparation is an action or process that is done to get something ready for use or service.[21] Preparation comes from living intentionally in the present while looking ahead to the future. Abram had already had some significant encounters with God, and blessings as his flocks and herds grew, but God still hadn't given him the promised child or land. In the meantime, all he could do was wait on God. And he didn't just passively wait; he prepared.

Abram probably didn't expect a war to sweep through his region, or for his nephew to be captured. When he moved to Mamre, it could have been tempting to spend all his time building up his herds and flocks, or relaxing and trying for a baby with Sarai. Maybe Abram thought Mamre would be his safe 'forever home.' As he built alliances with his neighbors, he probably hoped that the biggest favor he'd ever have to call in would be asking his neighbors for help during shearing time. Maybe Abram expected to need help watching for a band of pesky camel thieves. Thankfully, none of that happened. Abram trained his own private army to be ready to protect the animals and families, and help his neighbors if needed.

Preparation had been worked out on the daily in Abram's life. It had also been worked out in the lives of the people under Abram's care. Before Abram even knew what the outcome was to his life and future, how he would have a child or how they would possess the land, Abram did the hard and long work of preparation. All of it started at the trees of Mamre, and would help him in the years ahead.

2. Preparation Led to Abram's Protection

And he [Abram] and his servants deployed against them by night, defeated them, and pursued them as far as Hobah to the north of Damascus. He brought back all the goods and also his relative Lot and his goods, as well as the women and the other people.
Genesis 14:15-16

Abram went into battle prepared, and God moved in a mighty way. God gave Abram discernment and wisdom, He helped Abram know how to divide the men and to defeat the opponents. Like other famous battles in history, size was no guarantee of success—the smaller army routed the larger enemy army completely! Abram and his men rescued Lot, the captured possessions, and the people.

Immediately after Abram got back from battle, two kings came out to meet him. One with a blessing and one with a temptation. Once again, Abram's preparation helped him, this time to navigate a tricky situation with wisdom and discernment. Let's meet the two kings.

After Abram returned from defeating Chedorlaomer and the kings who were with him, the king of Sodom went out to meet him in the Shaveh Valley (that is, the King's Valley). Melchizedek, king of Salem, brought out bread and wine; he was a priest to God Most High.
Genesis 14:17-18

Who are these kings and what did they want? The first king, the one from Sodom, was one of the kings that Abram delivered during battle. He wanted to "pay" Abram back by dividing up the plunder from the battle. It's not hard to figure out who the king of Sodom was or his focus following the battle. He wanted to bargain with Abram!

The second king is different. He appeared out of nowhere. He was the king of Salem. Who was he and what did he want? There are two theories. Some people think this was an appearance on earth of the pre-incarnate Jesus (also known as a theophany). Other people believe that the king of Salem was an actual king who worshiped the One True God, and in a sense, represented Jesus. There are strengths and weaknesses for the different schools of thought. What we do know is that the king of Salem, named Melchizedek, represented God's way.[22]

I believe that when Abram was with God at Mamre, it helped him recognize the difference between the king of Sodom and the king of Salem. Why did Abram need protection in this situation when two different kings were trying to claim his attention? Because there are physical battles but also spiritual battles. Have you ever noticed that after a victory it's easy to get full of ourselves? We think we've got it together, and that it's OK to have a little bit of compromise in our lives.

Because Abram had gone through the preparation process at the trees of Mamre, he was not only ready for the physical battle but also for the spiritual battle in the following days. I love that God made sure Abram was spiritually, physically, and emotionally ready, so he could face the temptation that the king of Sodom put in front of him and be ready to respond to the king of Salem in worship.

God knows the battle before we get to the battle. He's preparing us based on what He knows is going to unfold.

3. Preparation Led to Abram's Focus

During the meeting with the kings, something significant happened. The king of Salem brought out bread and wine. This was an early picture of the Lord's Supper. The king of Salem spoke a blessing over Abram. Listen to what Melchizedek said.

> *Abram is blessed by God Most High,*
> *Creator of heaven and earth,*
> *and blessed be God Most High*
> *who has handed over your enemies to you.*
> Genesis 14:19b, 20

The blessing was clear. Abram did not deliver himself or his people from the battle; it was not Abram's trained men or his alliances that ultimately delivered anyone or anything. While God did work through the alliances, and He did work through the trained men, it was God who provided the victory. That's an important reminder for us in our spiritual, physical, and emotional battles. Abram worked hard. Abram trained hard. Abram was all in, but God provided the victory.

Abram responded to the king of Salem in a beautiful way. "And Abram gave him a tenth of everything" (Genesis 14:20). I see this as a moment of worship. This was another first in Scripture. Abram's offering of a tenth showed where his heart was, and where his loyalty lay. Many people believe the tithe was introduced in this encounter.[23] There was something special about this moment for Abram, so he gave sacrificially to Melchizedek.

From what we can see, Melchizedek didn't ask for anything. Abram just gave. God moved in Abram's life, and Abram responded by giving to God. It was a sign of a relationship established in love, trust, and commitment. When we give, we show our dependence on God trusting him to be our provider and protector.

Blessings can come in different ways. Here we see that God blessed

Abram with the wisdom to give and God was going to bless Abram with the wisdom to make a good choice. But, more than anything, God blessed Abram by being in a relationship with him.

4. *Preparation Led to Abram's Resolve*

In contrast, what did the king of Sodom want? *"Then the king of Sodom said to Abram, 'Give me the people, but take the possessions for yourself'" (Genesis 14:21).*

In today's terms, the king of Sodom was saying, "Let's make a deal. Let's enter into a partnership. You take the loot. I take the people. You win. I win." By human standards, it would have been a smart decision to collaborate with the king. Abram could have collected more power and resources, things the world tells us we need. By accepting the offer, he could have competed better with other neighbors jostling for grazing grounds and riches. But listen to Abram's reply, straight out of Scripture.

But Abram said to the king of Sodom, "I have raised my hand in an oath to the Lord, God Most High, Creator of heaven and earth, that I will not take a thread or sandal strap or anything that belongs to you, so you can never say, 'I made Abram rich.'"
Genesis 14:22-23

I love the resolve in Abram's voice. When Abram swore by God, and refused the bounty, I see this as another defining moment for Abram. Basically, Abram said to the king of Sodom, "I belong to the One True God. I'm not linking arms with you. Sodom, your story doesn't belong in my story."

Sometimes it helps to pull back the cultural curtain on a scene and know what was really at stake. Basically, if Abram had taken the bounty, bragging rights for Abram's later riches and blessings could have gone to the king of Sodom. God wouldn't have gotten the glory for what was to come in Abram's life.

What I think was telling is why Abram wasn't going to accept anything from the king of Sodom. The reason revealed what was going on in Abram's heart. Abram trusted God to build his legacy. Abram's life and legacy were built **to** God, **with** God, **for** God, and **through** God. We don't see this line-in-the-sand moment anywhere else in Abram's life where another king or leader could have had influence over Abram. Despite the offer from Sodom, Abram followed God's way, even though he didn't know how his future would unfold. Whether Abram knew it or not, this was a God-sized moment in his life that defined him (in a good way!) for the rest of his life.

Our Journey

I love a God-sized moment. I am here for it every single time! I want spiritual victory. I want a story that points to God and gives Him glory. Often where I fall short is in the day-in-and-day-out focus or preparation.

In the morning, I don't naturally wake up with Jesus as my first priority (that would be coffee). It's too easy for me to start answering messages, checking my calendar, or worrying about my day, instead of spending time with God. What helps is when I build a resolve in my life to meet with Jesus every morning. By cultivating focus and preparation in my daily rhythms, I make space for God to pour into me. Then I can pour my life out for Him. (And whether that happens before, during, or after my first cup of coffee doesn't matter.)

-Andrea

Lot had settled in a place that led to his captivity. Abram had settled in a place that provided peace. Yet, a battle still landed in Abram's lap. What a great picture of living in today's world! We try to do the right thing. We keep our eyes on the prize of Jesus, and boom, a battle lands in our lap. How can we be prepared? How can we remain focused? How can the battle lead to a God-sized moment in our lives?

As we focus on Jesus, we will see the God-sized moments in our lives. Often we miss them because of the details of life, the busyness, the distractions, the self-focus, and the daily spiritual battles. So many of us have testimonies that we think are boring or routine but think about the goodness of God. He makes a way for us to be in a relationship with Him and to be sustained by Him. We constantly allow familiarity or busyness to steal that truth from us. But every time we meet with God and He meets with us, we are prepared for battle and that preparation leads to God-sized moments!

1. Preparation Leads to Our Progress

Finish this thought. "If Abram spent time with God at the Trees of Mamre, I will spend time with God __." Some possible answers include: "in the morning," "on my lunch break," or "right before I go to bed." And those are great answers! We need that intentional, protected time to meet with God. But, the conversation needs to go a little deeper. "If Abram prepared for the day of battle by enjoying time with God, building alliances with others, and training his men for battle, I will prepare for my battles by__." Some possible answers include: "reading my Bible," "journaling my prayers," "memorizing Scripture," "singing songs of praise," or "sharing my faith." All of those can be turned into habits and rhythms! When we spend time with the Lord, He has the chance to shape and fill us. This helps us grow in maturity and wisdom in our faith.

Preparation also can mean surrounding ourselves with the right people. In God's family, we have built-in allies who love us, cheer for us, and challenge us as we serve together. While taking the time to focus on our private relationship with God is important, we were also meant to grow and learn in community. God created us to be in relationship with Him and one another. Abram could have gone into battle by himself...but he was stronger by joining with others. And so are we.

What are our daily rhythms that prepare us for our battle, or someone else's battle? Where was Abram and what was he doing? The answer to this question mattered for him, and it matters for us. The people we're around, the things we're doing, the season you're in—all of it matters. All of it is moving us closer to when God will show up and move.

Sometimes we have to do the hard work of walking obediently with God without knowing how things will turn out. Progress means we keep pressing on, we don't settle or stop. God is building the character and resources into us for whatever is ahead. He's building into us what we need, even when we don't know we need it!

2. Preparation Leads to Our Protection

We may not live in a war zone like Abram and Lot, but we need to be battle ready. We face a real enemy who has a battle plan and it is for our defeat. Some of us are in a battle right now. We are overwhelmed by spiritual attacks, we are overwhelmed by the circumstances going on in our lives. If that's the case for you, friend, just know that sometimes it's in the battle where God does the best preparation. So, dig deep into faith, dig deep into what God has for you. Put on the full armor of God from the top of your head to the bottom of your feet, so that you go into your battle protected. I have some good news for you! Your protection does not depend on you. Your protection is based on Jesus and what He did for you on the cross. And your protection is sealed by the work of the Holy Spirit in your life.

So, how are we going to navigate spiritual battles and spiritual warfare? Ephesians 6:10-18 tells us to be battle ready by putting on the full armor of God because the day of evil is coming. Do you have your spiritual armor in place?

- The belt of truth.
- The breastplate of righteousness.
- The Gospel shoes.

- The shield of faith.
- The helmet of salvation.
- The sword of the spirit.
- Praying in all situations.

There's always a war going on around us. Sometimes it's our battle, sometimes it's somebody else's battle. As New Testament believers we're not fighting for victory but from victory. Through Christ we already know the victory is coming, so we approach the battles differently. Preparation is connected to our time in the Word of God, it's connected to the people who are speaking truth into our lives, and it's connected to our resolve to live for the things of God. Putting on the full armor of God daily helps us meet the battle in God's strength, not our own.

3. Preparation Leads to Our Focus

What does clear focus look like in the middle of the battle? It looks like the blood of Christ offering ultimate victory over every battle we face. As we focus on Jesus, and His finished work on the cross, our focus changes from the temporary to the eternal. Then we see God for who He is and how He works, and it gives us that needed push to take the next faith step.

Abram focused on God by taking the bread and the wine with the king of Salem. We can do the same thing. Daily we can remember to think about what Jesus did for us on the cross. I will never get over what Jesus did for me on the cross. He took my place. He paid my debt. He satisfied God's penalty for my sin—Jesus' death. It's hard to think about, especially since Jesus didn't deserve to die. But, it was Jesus' death and His defeat of death that ultimately brought us victory.

When we look to Jesus and worship him, our lives change. Our focus changes. We see things through the lens of Jesus' finished work on the cross and it helps us know how to move forward in faith. "Lord, I'm not going to hold back from you. I'm going to be 'all in' when it comes to you because I know you're 'all in' when it comes to me!"

When we give to the Lord we show where our focus is. When we give, we remember that everything we have is God's. We're just stewards of what He's given us. We understand ownership. "I belong to God. My stuff belongs to God. My life belongs to God." Giving is trust, because God entrusted it to us, and we're giving it back to Him and His kingdom. Obviously, saving for retirement is good! What Abram was doing at this moment by giving a tenth to the king of Salem is a great example for us in our own lives. When God moves in our life, how do we give back to God?

And sometimes that will mean just giving our attention to the things of God by listening to someone on a busy day, or giving money to someone in need. Sometimes that will look like serving and volunteering in a place out of our comfort zone. Wherever we are in our journey, we can take the next step of faith and obedience. Let's pray that we never get comfortable. God-sized focus always moves us forward in our journey.

4. Preparation Leads to Our Resolve

One of the things we see in Abram's oath is how his vertical relationship with God affected his horizontal interactions with others. It opened up his perspective and opened up his choices. Abram was resolved to follow God. Because Abram knew how God saw him, it mattered less how others saw him. It mattered less if he didn't know the outcome of rejecting the offer from the king of Sodom. And that changed the choices Abram made. What about us, and our choices?

When I read about Abram's encounter after the battle, Abram's resolve inspires me. I see Abram telling the king of Sodom, "You don't get any part of what's going on in my life." It's like Abram was closing a door on something he knew was not part of God's plan for him, something that looked good but would just trap him.

In our lives, what doors do we need to close? Is there a media channel that you follow that tells you to be more of something or less of something? Do you have a friendship or relationship that consistently tempts you towards unhealthy choices? What about a negative environment where you're sucked into competition if you want to survive? Or a codependent relationship, where you're only valued for what you can do or give, and not for who you are? There are some voices and ideas that we need to deny space in our story. God has better plans for us as we journey! There are amazing times ahead when we'll get to see how our victory doesn't come from ourselves, or from the people, things, or circumstances around us. It will come from something that only God could do. That is a God-sized moment and the roots of those moments find their beginnings in the easy and not so easy choices we make.

Sometimes we want to know what will happen before we commit to something. We want instant results for any faith step, a sort of 'microwave Christianity.' When we don't see those instant results we doubt if God ever spoke to us at all, or whether He's real. Instead of trusting God until we see the outcome, we refuse to trust God unless we can see the outcome! Honestly, sometimes there are long seasons where we DON'T see the benefit of following God. And that's when preparing and resolving help us make the right choice anyway.

Transforming Truth:
Trusting God Leads to God-sized Moments.

> "Lord, we focus on You during this season of life. We trust You with the easy and not so easy choices we face. Thank You for teaching us. Thank You for showing us truths that apply to our everyday lives. Lord, may we be prepared for our battles and may we be focused on what really matters. Help us live intentionally in Your protection and Your provision and experience the blessing that You have for us. In Jesus' name, amen."

DISCUSSION QUESTIONS

As we journey through the life of Abraham, think about your life. What is God cultivating in you? How can faith and trust grow in your life? What is your greatest struggle? What is defining you in this season of your journey?

Chapter 4: God-sized Moments

1. Abram developed a friendship with God at the Trees of Mamre. How do you consistently build a friendship with God? What are your daily spiritual rhythms and routines?
2. Preparation for the day of battle was part of Abram's time at Mamre. Describe the role preparation plays in the lives of believers.
3. What role does preparation play in the discernment process? Abram was able to close the door on the King of Sodom and freely worship the King of Salem. Life is filled with choices between different paths and relationships. How do the people around us and our priorities set us up for success or failure?
4. Preparation is all about focus! What are you looking to and who are you looking for as you journey through life? Day-in-and-day-out, where is your focus?

I hope your answer is "on God" because all of us are going to have our Genesis 14 moments. We're going to face battles. Our friends and family will face battles. We're going to have to step into messy situations where there are power struggles, confusion, and divided alliances. And in those situations, we can choose to keep our eyes focused on God. When we do, we're going to experience God-sized moments.

This leads to our Transforming Truth: Trusting God leads to God-sized moments!

5. Share a God-sized moment in your life when you know God prepared you for the day of battle and victory was yours because of the way God prepared you and the way you responded by faith!

Chapter 5

Questions and Doubts

Questions and doubts. Everyone has them. In our hardest seasons, it's still possible to believe that God loves us. He is not mad at us for asking questions or struggling with doubts. He offers a safe place for us to be real. We can bring our real emotions and struggling perspectives to Him and trust Him to speak truth into our hearts. God can handle what is going on inside of us. Not only that, God understands it better than we do!

One thing we will see in Abram's journey is that he did not stay in the struggle. While Abram had real questions and doubts, they were not the end of his story. In fact, his questions and doubts provided a beautiful place for God to work in and through Abram's life. The same is true for you and me!

His Journey

Let's pick up in Genesis 15. Abram was living his life, doing his thing. Then the Lord appeared to him in a vision that brought up some questions and doubts. The questions were about the promise God had made to Abram about being the father of a great nation. The doubts were about God's willingness to fulfill the promise. God orchestrated things in a way that Abram's struggles came to the surface. Then God spoke truth into Abram's situation. We'll see how God brought up those questions and doubts and then entered into a covenant with Abram as a way to address them. So, let's jump into Genesis 15 and discover four key points, which will lead us to our transforming truth: *God is sure, He is steady, He is able!*

1. God Kept Showing Up

After these events, the word of the Lord came to Abram in a vision: Do not be afraid, Abram. I am your shield, your reward will be very great.
Genesis 15:1

I love how God kept showing up in Abram's life. Remember how God appeared to Abram in Genesis 12? That was when God called Abram to leave his homeland. God also called Abram to trust Him with his future and to believe God could—and would—establish him as the father of a great nation (Genesis 12:1-3). Time passed and Abram was still waiting on the fulfillment of the promise. I'm sure Abram had highs and lows during the waiting process. Maybe he wondered if he blew it. Maybe he wondered if he had disqualified himself. Maybe he wondered if God really meant the promise in the first place!

God knew there were some deep struggles in Abram's heart, maybe better than Abram did himself. So, when God showed up this time He said, "Do not be afraid." The word afraid used in Genesis 15 has two meanings. The meaning used in this context is, "to have an emotional or intellectual anticipation of harm or danger." It also means "to have a sense of dread."[24] It's easy to struggle with dread or fear, especially after a difficult season. Remember, Abram had been through a lot in Genesis 14, with the first recorded battle in the Bible. There is something about a battle—physical, emotional, or spiritual—that sticks with us long after the battle is over. It's also easy to struggle with dread or fear when waiting on the fulfillment of a promise. The instruction, "Do not be afraid," was really about the character of God more than about Abram's circumstances. God gave Abram two reasons why he should not fall into the trap of fear.

First, God reminded Abram that it was God's job to be Abram's shield. God was the one who would protect, provide, and care for Abram. Second, God said He would make Abram's reward great. The New International Version Bible translation even gives the idea of God being the actual reward. I love that! Yes, there are all kinds of earthly blessings and experiences, but they all fall short of ultimately meeting our greatest need.

God made a bold promise and He made a bold proclamation. In the process, it brought up a question and a doubt for Abram.

2. God Listened to Abram's Doubts

But Abram said, "Lord God, what can you give me, since I am childless and the heir of my house is Eliezer of Damascus?" Abram continued, "Look, you have given me no offspring; so a slave born in my house will be my heir."
Genesis 15:2-3

In two verses, Abram put everything on the table. He shared his honest question and deep doubt. Sometimes the Bible is silent on the thoughts and feelings of the people in it. We can only guess how they were processing a situation. Verses like Genesis 15:2-3 pack a powerful punch because we not only see the struggle, but we can also feel it.

In Genesis 15, Abram had a big question about two big promises. One promise dealt with *land*, which was going to be fulfilled with the Promised Land. The other promise dealt with legacy, which was going to be fulfilled with the birth of Isaac. Land issues and legacy issues are two themes that run throughout the Old Testament, and there's a reason why.

The land was crucial because God was carving out a place for His chosen people, the nation of Israel. It was a prime spot of land that God had promised to Abram. God was going to give it—hundreds of years later—to Abram's descendants after their long stay in Egypt and a trying trip through the desert.

Legacy was also important because it was through the descendants of Abram that Jesus would come. God raised up a nation to provide a lineage, and through that lineage there would be authenticating factors for the Messiah. Once the Messiah was here, people with questions and doubts could go back through God's story and see how every promise made by God was kept by God. That is why the gospel of Matthew opens with a genealogy leading directly from Abram to the birth of Jesus. Everything that happened in Genesis 15 was setting the stage for Jesus to come. But Abram didn't know any of that in Genesis 15. And it probably seemed like there was no way God could answer the question:"What can You give me?" I hear such a sense of hopelessness in Abram's question. It seems to echo a previous struggle in Abram's life when he was dealing with the lies of the enemy and the lies of the flesh during his days in Egypt.

3. God Met Abram in his Questions

How would God respond to Abram? A big part of me thinks Abram wanted to hold on to faith despite the questions and doubts. If so, Abram had to be willing to listen to God's reply. He had to turn his heart to the Lord and be open for the Lord to speak truth to him.

> *Now the word of the Lord came to him: "This one will not be your heir; instead, one who comes from your own body will be your heir." He took him outside and said, "Look at the sky and count the stars, if you are able to count them." Then he said to him, "Your offspring will be that numerous."*
> *Genesis 15:4-5*

God certainly answered Abram's question! The answer was clear and to the point. And it led to a moment of decision. Was Abram going to believe God or was Abram going to hold onto his own perspective? We see a very clear answer from Abram. In verse six, after God said to go and look at the stars, what did Abram do?

> *Abram believed the Lord, and he credited it to him as righteousness.*
> *Genesis 15:6*

Abram had faith! As far as we can tell, Abram didn't ask a ton of questions or try to figure out when it might happen. The Bible says Abram believed God. Abram's faith was the key to victory in his life, and faith is key to victory in our lives! Whenever we read Genesis 15:6, that is a crucial Bible verse! We might wonder, "How were Old Testament believers justified before God? How were they made right before God in comparison to New Testament believers?" And this verse levels the playing field. It has always been by faith! Just like us, they had to trust God and believe God by choosing his way over their way. Abram asked a question, God responded with a promise, and Abram believed God. But God didn't just give lip service to Abram's worries through this promise. He took it a step further.

4. God's Covenant with Abram

Abram had faith; he trusted God. But that didn't mean all his doubts and worries were gone. There was another question that needed to be asked and answered. Once again, God initiated the process of bringing the question to the surface. Check out what God said to Abram!

> *He also said to him, "I am the Lord who brought you from Ur of the Chaldeans to give you this land to possess." But he said, "Lord God, how can I know that I will possess it?"*
> *Genesis 15:7-8*

I love how one question ("What about the child?") led to another question ("What about the land?") in Abram's life as God reminded Abram where their journey began in Ur. Back then, God appeared to Abram and said, "Go from your land, your relatives, and your father's house to the land that I will show you" (Genesis 12:1). Years later, God was willing to bring up the promise of the land and deal with the question Abram had about it.

That's the beauty of God. His work isn't surface-level work. It's deep work, it's penetrating work. It's work that goes down to the difficult situations and circumstances going on in life. As questions surfaced, God reminded Abram that He was faithful to provide exactly what Abram needed. God was with Abram and God was for Abram. Next, God told Abram to bring animals for a sacrifice, as part of a formal agreement, or covenant. Once the animals had been offered, God spoke to Abram again.

> He said to him, "Bring me a three-year-old cow, a three-year-old female goat, a three-year-old ram, a turtledove, and a young pigeon." So he brought all these to him, cut them in half, and laid the pieces opposite each other, but he did not cut the birds in half. Birds of prey came down on the carcasses, but Abram drove them away. As the sun was setting, a deep sleep came over Abram, and suddenly great terror and darkness descended on him. Then the Lord said to Abram, "Know this for certain: Your offspring will be resident aliens for four hundred years in a land that does not belong to them and will be enslaved and oppressed. However, I will judge the nation they serve, and afterward they will go out with many possessions. But you will go to your ancestors in peace and be buried at a good old age."
> —Genesis 15:9-15

This is called the Abrahamic Covenant, and it later became a cornerstone of Jewish faith. In the Bible, we see that God used covenants to move His story forward; His covenants were personal and rooted in a relationship.[25] We see this in His covenants with Adam, Noah, Moses, and David, for example, and then the New Covenant through Jesus. We're not going to go deep into the covenant, but it's helpful for us to know what the Abrahamic Covenant was, why God used it, and what we can take away from it. God was predicting how Abram's descendants would come out of captivity in Egypt. They would travel to the Promised Land, becoming a unified nation along the way, and settle there as a nation with one God. God and Abram entered into a covenant, and at that moment, it was a done deal.

Usually in books, Bible studies, or messages covering Genesis 15, there's a deep dive into the covenant. Our focus in this book is different. This is a deep dive into God speaking truth into Abram's life. Abram had questions. God had answers. Out of that, a covenant was established. The heart of God was on display as He spoke into the struggles in Abram's life.

Our Journey

> When I was a teenager I started taking walks late at night to spend time with God. I called them 'goodnight walks.' I would walk and think through my day, and I was always encouraged when I looked up at the stars and remembered Abraham's story. God had promised him that his descendants would be as numerous as the stars in the sky. I knew God was making promises to me. The stars were like a reminder to keep putting one foot in front of the other. It helped me to know that there was a bigger story than

what I could understand or see. To this day my 'goodnight walks' with God shape my spiritual focus. I am reminded that my walk with God during my time on this earth has a beginning, and an ending, and every step in the middle matters. Just like the stars reminded Abram of God's promises, the stars remind me of God's faithfulness on my own journey.

-Andrea

Facing our questions and doubts, helps us look at who God is and how He works. When God reveals himself to us during seasons of struggle, we learn to trust Him instead of our circumstances, and our faith grows. No matter where we are in the journey, God is faithful to make a way.

What strikes me in Genesis 15 is the heart of God. God saw Abram in his struggle, and God did not leave him there. God was willing to share truth with Abram. Then, He confirmed the truth with a covenant. God saw Abram. God loved Abram. God was with Abram. God helped Abram even if Abram didn't know he was struggling with questions and doubts. That's the God we serve, and He is doing the same thing for us!

1. *God Keeps Showing Up*

Sometimes we forget how often God shows up in our lives. That is the thing about questions and doubts—they can nag at us and cause us to expect more trouble. Instead of expecting things to level out, we expect the bottom to fall out. Sometimes it's because we think we deserve bad things. Other times we think God is out to get us. We look around and think there's no way God can turn our situation around. "What if God doesn't come through with what He promised me?" The questions and doubts swirl in our hearts and minds.

Through it all, God protects us by showing up again and again and again. It's not wrong to have questions. It's good, and it's healthy. But it has to come under the authority of knowing that God is our shield and reward. His plan is evidence of His goodness in our lives. Sometimes we don't even recognize a struggle until God reveals it to us or someone speaks into our lives. Maybe we've normalized the struggle, or we haven't had to really face it. Genesis 15 was a pivotal chapter in the story, where Abram's faith was verbalized in a real way. Faith came in the middle of the struggle. Here is what we have to understand. Abram's reward or shield wasn't the child or the land, it was God. We want to make the destination the most important part of our story—like Abram's child or the Promised Land. But God is saying, "All along the way, I'll be the reward, I'll be the shield. I am the point of the journey." Whenever we get to the place of faith, we realize that God is the one who keeps showing up. And in the context of our questions, God is the pathway through our questions. When we understand that, we experience God as our shield and reward.

If you're waiting on a promise, or a resolution, in a season of waiting, watch and see how God keeps showing up. No one and nothing can ever take from you that God is your shield and your reward. That's the beauty of the relationship we have with God through Christ.

In Genesis 15:1, God made a promise to Abram that counts for us too. Do you believe that God is willing to be your shield and your reward in your own life? God is saying to you, "Do not be afraid, do not dread the future. I am your shield, I am protecting you. I am going before you, I am making a way for you." In the face of overwhelming situations, do we grasp that God is the one providing safety and protection for us? Yes, there are all kinds of physical blessings, experiences, and relationships, but all of them fall short of ultimately meeting our greatest need. At the end of the day, God is the one who we ultimately long for and He is the one that makes our reward great.

All of us have a unique relational space in our lives created by God and for God. As created beings, we were made to be in a relationship with our Creator. We try to fill this space with many things. Sometimes it's people or experiences. Maybe it's status or even wealth. Sometimes we try to fill it by trying to control our lives or to control others.

Knowing Jesus and walking with Him in intimacy is what satisfies. With that in place, we can enjoy everything else God gives us, like wonderful relationships, opportunities, and experiences. "Reward" is not an 'either/or' type of thing when it comes to God and earthly comforts or experiences. "Reward" really can be a 'both/and' type of thing when we understand that it's God who satisfies and God who provides. He is the one who meets the needs in our lives, in so many different ways. Sometimes we have to wait. Sometimes what we want and what we get don't always line up. But, in the midst of the waiting process, God is our shield and God is our reward. And ultimately that's how we get our questions resolved.

2. *God Listens to Our Doubts*

Maybe you are there right now. Wondering. Doubting. Barely hanging on to faith. If so, I hope this truth flows over you like a fresh breeze on a hot day. ***God can handle your questions and doubts.*** God will not be surprised by one thing you say or one thing you think or feel. In fact, He already knows and understands the issues swirling in your head. Maybe, like Abram, you've messed up. Do you need to hear that you haven't blown it, you're not without hope or help? When you're wondering how to navigate your challenges, God is whispering, "I am here for you!"

We may tell ourselves to just try harder, just read our Bible more, and just be a better Christian, hoping it will help. We may push ourselves to be more committed, but God is always committed to us! Like Abram, what if we bring our questions and deep doubts to God? Sometimes the first step is to be honest with ourselves so we can be honest with the Lord. This can get messy because we're so used to trying to have the "right answers" or to pray the "right prayers" for wisdom, guidance, etc. Sometimes we have to be gut-level honest and just admit the struggle in our lives by saying, "God. I am not OK right now."

As hard as it is, when we get real about our faith (or lack of faith!), our faith actually grows! It may take several reminders to ourselves that the Lord already knows and He can handle anything. This may bring up a question: "Since He already knows it all, is there any point in bringing our questions to the Lord?" Absolutely. That's how we get real about life and get real on our journey. That's how we open up a conversation where we can communicate with God, just like in any other relationship in our lives. If you're struggling, God offers a safe place for you to be real and honest. In fact, God wants you to be honest! Honesty leads to God speaking direction, hope, and truth into our situations and circumstances.

Most of the time we know the places in life where we're hurting. We know where we're struggling. But here's an important question: Are we open to a new perspective? Are we open to God's Word being real or clarifying during questions and doubts? You don't have to hold back and you don't have to try to clean yourself up in order to come to God. Look up at the stars tonight and remember the same God who spoke so tenderly to Abram still speaks to us!

3. God Meets Us in Our Questions

One of the things we see repeated in Abram's story is how God kept connecting with him. God kept reaffirming His promise and purpose for Abram. *"I'm still with you, we're still doing this thing. I promise this is going to happen."* Abram had questions and doubts, and there was tension when Abram talked with God. But there was also reaffirmation—the land and the child would come in God's timing and God's way, according to God's will and God's plan. God was walking with Abram, and God is walking with us.

Remember how we talked about going back to our Bethel? Going back to a place—in our memory or in real life—where God spoke into our lives? There are these standout moments that do two things. They show the way in the moment, but they also encourage us later, and reaffirm God's presence in seasons of waiting and wondering.

When we read a story like Abram's, we may want to get it to a good place, a neat, tidy resolution. And we want the same for our own struggles! But when we try to force 'our' resolution, we can miss the bigger thing God's doing. That's something to remember—the way resolution looks for us and for Him are different. Our resolution doesn't have to be in a perfect set of circumstances. Our resolution is in Christ. That helps us navigate whatever the story turns out to be.

God provides exactly what we need, exactly when we need it, even if we can't see it at the time. There are some truths that are crucial for us to know as New Testament believers so that when the questions and doubts surface—and they will—we are ready to respond in faith.

- God sent Jesus to secure our salvation. This gives us victory over the grave.
- God sent the Holy Spirit to be our guide. This gives us daily victory over sin.
- God gave us the Bible so we can know how to live. This gives us victory over confusion, shame, doubt, and fear.
- God gave us the church, our faith family, so we are not alone. This gives us victory over isolation and loneliness.

God meets us in our questions and doubts with truth. Sometimes we have to wait on God's timing over our timing. Waiting is really hard and usually means questions and doubts will start to surface. Through the waiting process, though, we figure out what we want *in* life and what we want *out of* life. God uses waiting to help us see what our end goal really is. And anytime we can get down to the nitty-gritty when it comes to our walk with God, that's what brings spiritual fruit!

4. God's Covenant with Us

Genesis 15:6 says, "Abram believed the Lord, and he credited it to him as righteousness." How does that happen in our lives? The same way it happened in Abram's life—*by faith!* The moment we believe God, and accept His way instead of our way, He changes our lives.

Let's talk about our journey and how every step is guided by a promise-making and promise-keeping God. I don't think anyone has ever asked me, *"Where are you on your faith journey?"* And yet, if they had asked me, it could have brought focus and clarity during seasons of questions and doubts. Since our faith journey as believers can be complicated, it helps to divide it into 'stages' of progress: salvation, sanctification, and glorification. We may see a mess of mistakes and doubts and dry seasons, but God sees a beautiful ongoing work of redemption! And, man, does that bring perspective to what our time on earth is all about.

- **Salvation** means coming to faith in Jesus Christ. If we've placed our faith in Jesus for the forgiveness of our sins, we've moved from spiritual death to spiritual life. We are believers in Jesus Christ, and we are children of God. Salvation is a crucial step in our spiritual journey. You can't move on without it, but it's not the ending point!
- Salvation leads to **sanctification**, which is becoming more like Jesus and less like this world. The sanctification part means we are willing to be changed or transformed in the everyday parts of life so that we reflect Jesus. It is easy to forget about the sanctification part of our journey. Sometimes we just coast through this particular season of our time here on this earth, getting distracted and caught up in everyday life. Because sin is real, and we tend to get lazy and fall into sinful patterns, we can get off track. But every day brings the chance to reset. Sanctification is an exciting adventure to lay down our lives and follow Jesus…every single day!
- One day our time on this earth will come to an end. I hope that's encouraging to you because this world is not our home. As we live with our eyes focused on Jesus in the sanctification part of our journey, it prepares us for **glorification**. This is the moment when we will go home to heaven to be with God for all of eternity.

The reason I bring this up is because just like Abram, we are on a journey. In Genesis 15, in the middle of questions and doubts, God clarified Abram's journey, and He will do the same for you and me.

My challenge for you is to think about where you are in your walk with God. Maybe you're reading this book and you've never placed your faith in Jesus. Maybe you've been trying all the good things, you've been trying to rely on yourself. But today is a chance for you to turn from trusting in yourself and to place your faith in Jesus for the forgiveness of your sins, to experience **salvation**. How can you be saved? By confessing your sin, admitting your need for a Savior, and placing your trust in Jesus' death and resurrection. You can pray right now, no matter where you are, and ask Jesus to save you! The moment you do, so many questions and doubts will be resolved in your life.

If you have already placed your faith in Jesus, you are a child of God! **Sanctification** is where it is at for you. That is that process of daily asking the Lord, "How can I look like you, act like you, and respond like you? How can I navigate my battle in a way that is intentional and ultimately results in your glory, God?" When you get the answer from God's Word or from His leading in your life, do it!

Every day we can become more like Jesus—that's our daily opportunity, friend. I'm so excited about sanctification for you and for me, especially in the areas of life filled with questions and doubts. This is one of the most challenging but also most rewarding stages because we need God's help as we grow and change. His Word and His Spirit help us transform into His image in ways we never expected. Last of all, sanctification leads to **glorification**, the moment when we leave this world and enter our eternal home with God in heaven. Questions and doubts will be long gone, and faith will finally be sight!

▶▶▶ Transforming Truth: ◀▶

God is sure, He is steady, He is able!

"Lord, we love You so much, and we thank You for Your word, and how Your word encourages us. Maybe we're in our waiting season, maybe in the midst of our questions and doubts, Lord. We thank You that You already know full well what's going on in each of our individual lives, and there's not one thing that takes You by surprise, and there's not one thing that is too hard for You. There's not one thing that leaves You guessing or wondering where we should go from here. Right now, we bring our questions to You. We bring our doubts to You. We know that You are a safe place for us to be real and to be open and to be honest. Father, we will see You as sure, as steady, as able, as loving, as capable, in the midst of our own situations. We are open to You speaking truth and bringing the clarity we need. In Jesus' name, amen."

DISCUSSION QUESTIONS

As we journey through the life of Abraham, think about your life. What is God cultivating in you? How can faith and trust grow in your life? What is your greatest struggle? What is defining you in this season of your journey?

Chapter 5: Questions and Doubts

1. Do you believe God can handle your questions and doubts? Do you trust that God offers a "safe place" for you to bring the struggles going on in your life?
2. God told Abram, "Do not be afraid." How does fear impact our ability to trust God?
3. Abram was honest about his questions and doubts. He poured out his heart to the Lord. A great way to do this is to journal our real feelings and honest prayers. Another way to do this is by talking to the Lord out loud as we drive down the road or walk around the block. This brings up an important question. Do you tend to stuff your feelings or do you process them in real time?
4. Abram was open to a new perspective as a result of his honest conversation with the Lord. Are you open to a new perspective from the Lord regarding your questions and doubts? If so, here is an important question to consider. What do faith and trust look like in your area of struggle(s)?

This leads to our Transforming Truth: God is sure, He is steady, He is able!

5. God made a covenant with Abram and God made a covenant with us. We understand our covenant through the words salvation, sanctification, and glorification. Where are you on your faith journey? How does God's work in the past encourage you to trust him in the present and future?

Chapter 6

The God Who Sees

Abram had ups and downs, and he experienced twists and turns in life. He had mountaintop experiences where he believed God and he had valley experiences filled with questions and doubts. Through it all, God was faithful. The promise of Isaac and the Promised Land was safe and secure in God's heart. In Genesis 15 we focused on Abram's questions and doubts, how God reassured Him, and what faith looked like in Abram's life.

And then, boom! We land in Genesis 16. In our day, this would sound like a bad reality show. But in that context, children were so important, and the role of women was different. Still, Genesis 16 is hard to read. It was even harder for Abram, Sarai, and a new woman to live. However, I will always be thankful that the Bible records it all. There is something helpful about seeing our heroes of the faith in their struggles and questions, as well as in their moments of clarity and focus. The whole story helps fortify us for our own journey.

His Journey

Remember in Genesis 15, we left Abram in this beautiful place of faith, and the establishment of the Abrahamic Covenant. Then some time later we find Abram in the place of struggle and the place of sin, as his past caught up with him. God's heart for the least likely will shine bright as we learn that God is the God who sees. Hang on, this is going to be a ride! Let's look at Genesis 16, where we will discover four key points, leading to our transforming truth: **God sees, He knows, and He cares.**

1. Abram's Broken World

Abram's wife, Sarai, had not borne any children for him, but she owned an Egyptian slave named Hagar.
Genesis 16:1

This verse reminds us of the problem going on in the lives of Abram and Sarai. There was no son! When problems happen, it's all too tempting to come up with human solutions instead of asking God for help and following His plan. And the human solution was exactly what happened in Genesis 16.

> *Sarai said to Abram, "Since the Lord has prevented me from bearing children, go to my slave; perhaps through her I can build a family."*
> *Genesis 16:2*

Who was this Egyptian woman? We know her name was Hagar. Many Bible scholars think that Hagar was introduced into Abram and Sarai's lives while they were in Egypt trying to escape the famine in Cannan.[26] Remember how Abram lied about his relationship with Sarai by saying she was his sister instead of his wife? God sent consequences, and Pharaoh sent Abram packing. Abram acquired menservants and maidservants while in Egypt, possibly including Hagar. No matter when she joined the family, we see that the interactions with Hagar had huge consequences for Abram and Sarai's relationship and their lives.

Sarai's mindset was clear in Genesis 16. "Since the Lord has prevented me from having a child...." Let's stop right there. I wish I could know for sure what was going on in Sarai's mind. It seems like Sarai was telling Abram what was missing from her life, and even blaming God for it. When Sarai suggested a solution, Abram agreed with her plan instead of walking in fortified faith like he did in Genesis 15.

> *So Abram's wife, Sarai, took Hagar, her Egyptian slave, and gave her to her husband, Abram, as a wife for him. This happened after Abram had lived in the land of Canaan ten years. He slept with Hagar, and she became pregnant.*
> *Genesis 16:3-4*

Abram took Hagar as his wife. Here it's important to understand that in the culture of that day, it was normal, even expected, for men to have multiple wives. But I believe that Hagar was never God's plan for Abram; that was Sarai's plan, and Abram went along with it. God's plan was always for Abram and Sarai to have a child that came from the promise and provision of God. That's a great lesson for us. There are things that happen in our world today but that does not make it right with God. Our broken world causes our relationships to be very complex.

> *When she [Sarai] saw that she [Hagar] was pregnant, her mistress became contemptible to her. Then Sarai said to Abram, "You are responsible for my suffering! I put my slave in your arms, and when she saw that she was pregnant, I became contemptible to her. May the Lord judge between me and you."*
> *Genesis 16:4-5*

Childbearing in Sarai's time and culture was one of the main ways a woman proved her value; the more children—especially sons—the better! Since Sarai was not able to have a child, and Hagar was, a power struggle developed between the two women, and Abram was caught in the middle of it. Along the way, no one asked God about the plan He had for them and their promised child. Abram and Sarai made a choice that made sense to them. Their choice led to conflict… and they didn't handle that in a godly way either. Imagine the dynamic between Sarai and Hagar. What could have been a sisterly bond, or at least a sort of teamwork situation, became a competition. The pregnant Hagar despised Sarai, empowered by her 'winning' circumstance and Sarah's 'losing' circumstance. But Sarai, as the senior wife, fought back, blaming Abram for the entire situation.

Abram replied to Sarai, "Here, your slave is in your power; do whatever you want with her." Then Sarai mistreated her so much that she ran away from her.
Genesis 16:6

While Hagar despised Sarai, Sarai mistreated Hagar. Sarai was the one who ultimately had the power because she was the primary wife, and she took advantage of that. As far as we can tell, Abram just withdrew from the situation, telling Sarai that she was in control of Hagar; so, Sarai could handle the situation however she wanted to handle it. The mistreatment of Hagar became so intense that Hagar ran away from Sarai. Maybe she was trying to go back to her homeland of Egypt; maybe she just wanted to go anywhere as long as she could get away from such a hopeless and broken situation where she felt stuck and mistreated.

2. God Asked a Question

The angel of the Lord found her [Hagar] by a spring in the wilderness, the spring on the way to Shur. He said, "Hagar, slave of Sarai, where have you come from and where are you going?" She replied, "I'm running away from my mistress Sarai."
Genesis 16:7-8

While Hagar was running, God was pursuing. Hagar found herself sitting by a spring of water when an angel showed up and talked to her. Some people believe the angel was Jesus. Others believe it was an angel of the Lord who came as a picture of what Jesus was going to do for us. Either way, the encounter was beautiful. In the midst of the brokenness, there was a redemption plan. *Hagar was never without hope.*

The angel of the Lord found Hagar near a spring in the desert…that's important, so hang onto that fact. The question the angel asked was a clarifying question. "Hagar, what's going on in your life? Hagar, what are you trying to accomplish by being out here in the desert?" The question gave Hagar the chance to think about her situation and give an answer. Hagar gave an honest reply. She was running away.

> *The angel of the Lord said to her, "Go back to your mistress and submit to her authority."*
> *Genesis 16:9*

I'm sure that wasn't what Hagar wanted to hear during a heavenly encounter. Sometimes it's easier to run and hide than to face our problems. But the instruction to go back wasn't the only thing the angel of the Lord had to say.

> *The angel of the Lord said to her, "I will greatly multiply your offspring, and they will be too many to count." The angel of the Lord said to her, "You have conceived and will have a son. You will name him Ishmael, for the Lord has heard your cry of affliction. This man will be like a wild donkey. His hand will be against everyone, and everyone's hand will be against him; he will settle near all his relatives."*
> *Genesis 16:10-12*

Hagar must have cried out to the Lord as she fled Sarai—crying out for help and deliverance. She was in a miserable situation that seemed hopeless. Sitting by the spring of water, probably the last thing she expected was for Abram's God to show up and talk to her. But that is exactly what happened.

The angel of the Lord was honest with Hagar. When you are pregnant you want the warm wishes to be just that...warm! But here's what we need to notice: *the angel of the Lord told the truth.* There was no trickery or manipulation. Who knows how many times Abram had retold the story of God promising him a son? Maybe Hagar had hoped that it was her child who would be the child of the promise. But at this moment, Hagar received her own promise. Her son would also lead to a multitude of descendants, but he would be constantly involved in conflicts. What God said through the angel was probably hard for Hagar to hear, but this honest encounter was life-giving to the runaway slave.

3. God Spoke into the Brokenness

> *So she named the Lord who spoke to her: "You are El-roi," for she said, "In this place, have I actually seen the one who sees me?"*
> *Genesis 16:13*

Hagar knew she had brokenness in her life. She knew she lived in a broken world. But Hagar also knew that God was speaking into her brokenness with the truth. Hagar recognized that she was catching a glimpse of the God who sees.

A beautiful thread throughout the Bible is a life-giving encounter at a spring of water, a river of water, or a deep well. So Hagar being at the spring was significant because it points to God's redemptive path and redemptive ability even in the brokenness of life.

The name 'El-roi' means 'the God who sees' or 'the God of sight.' "The God who knows everything and cares, the God who never misses a human step or heart-cry."[27] Hagar was seen by God and then she made a bold statement. It's like she was shouting, "God sees someone like me!" That's what Genesis 16 is all about. Yes, it was messy. Yes, it was hard. But it didn't stop the plan of God. God had a plan for every single person in the journey. The developments in Genesis 16 gave God a new way to show His truth, as life went on for Abram and Sarai and Hagar.

The story of Hagar is hard, it really is. It seems like it's not fair. We want to change it in some way. Or maybe we want to hit the pause button and say, "Abram, don't go this direction!" or "Sarai, don't believe that!" or "Hagar, don't do that!" While we can't do that, we can learn from it. We can see the faithfulness of God to see, to know, to redeem, and to restore any and every situation—no matter how broken it is.

4. A Chance to Start Again

So Hagar gave birth to Abram's son, and Abram named his son (whom Hagar bore) Ishmael. Abram was eighty-six years old when Hagar bore Ishmael to him.
Genesis 16:15-16

Instead of going to Egypt where it might have been easier for her, Hagar went back to Abram and Sarai. She went back to their household and gave birth to Ishmael, and raised him there. Hagar had the chance to go back to the very place she was running from and reflect the truth from her encounter with God. That's what happens when we have an encounter with God, even in the midst of the sin and the pain. We get a chance to go back and start again, even in broken situations, because of the God who sees!

Sarai and Hagar had created a toxic living environment together, but hopefully they were able to make peace with the situation after Hagar's return. As Abram's son, Ishmael would have had rights and privileges of his own, and some of that may have carried over to Hagar. Maybe the encounter with the angel gave Hagar a sense of self-worth so she didn't need to despise Sarah or flaunt her own child. Hagar had the chance to break that negative cycle in Abram's household by her own behavior, not by shaming Sarai or flaunting Ishmael.

Throughout the Bible, we see real people caught in dangerous or unhealthy circumstances outside their control. Think of Joseph sold into slavery, David fighting in wars, and Paul being thrown in jail. Living by faith in a broken situation outside of our control is something that is relevant throughout the Bible. What we don't see is a call to deliberately remain in a situation of one-sided bullying or abuse.

Hagar returned to Abram and Sarai, but the situation wasn't magically resolved when she walked in the door (or tent flap). Hagar stepped back into the situation of brokenness, sin, and power struggles. It wasn't automatically fixed; everyone had to keep navigating the messy and difficult situation. Three adults and a child, living in the same household—that had its own dynamic of good days and bad days, challenges and friction. And the next chapter of Genesis—chapter 17—happened fourteen years after Hagar went back. That was fourteen years of waiting and wondering for Abram, and it was fourteen years of navigating a messy situation for their entire family.

We don't know about Hagar's relationship with God, but the chance to start again and be a part of God's story is something we can learn from her. Remember, Abram, Sarai, and Hagar were real people who were living in real time. They didn't know how their story would end. They couldn't flip the page and read the next chapter. They had to reset when they messed up. But even through all their friction and struggle, God was faithful to show up on the landscape of their lives and speak truth. God saw each one of them and ministered to each heart living in a broken world. Thankfully, He does the same for us. He is the God who sees, knows, and cares

Our Journey

I was a newborn baby, waiting in the hospital for a family. I don't know many of the details but I do know that several sets of adoption papers were filled out for me. There was a question that haunted my heart for years, "Who was in the nursery window?" At the heart of this question was a much deeper question. "God, do You see me?" I was a helpless baby in need of rescue. God sent my parents to rescue and adopt me. I am so thankful that He is the God who sees.

-Andrea

1. Our Broken World

Centuries later, our world hasn't gotten much brighter. There are two things at play in this reality. Brokenness happens to us and around us, but we also act out of our own sin and shame. Sin is any wrong thought, action, or reaction that does not line up with God and His perfect standard (Psalm 139:23-24). The Bible states in Romans 3:23 that everyone has sinned—which includes me, you, Abram, and Sarai! To this day, there's still hurt and betrayal, negativity and rejection.

Sometimes the brokenness comes from our own choices. Sometimes the brokenness comes from others' choices. And sometimes the brokenness comes from a blend of both. But even in a world that is messy, and overwhelmed by compromise and sin, God is on His throne. The pain, trouble, and brokenness open a door for God's redeeming work.

Sarai had deep pain from being childless, but she chose to mistreat Hagar and blame God, instead of pouring out her pain to God. Abram had his own questions for God, but from what we can see, he passively let the women in his household fight it out around him. Hagar was being mistreated, but she also mistreated Sarai in her own way and then left for the desert.

Let's jump ahead a few centuries from Abram's time, to Jesus talking with another woman at a well. "Jesus said, 'Everyone who drinks from this water will get thirsty again. But whoever drinks from the water that I will give him will never get thirsty again" *(John 4:13-14)*.

When we take the time to sit by the spring of Life, we start to see ourselves the way He sees us. Do we believe that Jesus sees us in our brokenness and in our pain? Do we believe that He is willing to lead us and guide us from the broken place? Friend, that is who He is and that is how He works. He provides the full life. He provides the free life. Even in the midst of sin and brokenness, *Jesus has the answer because He is the answer.* Your doubt, sin, hurt, regret, or shame does not have to define your life. God is able to redeem and restore!

2. God Asks a Question

Can you relate to Hagar? Do you wonder if God sees you? Even if He does see you, does He care that you're in that desert? The angel of the Lord found Hagar next to a spring of water, in the middle of the desert. From Genesis to Revelation, springs of water are a metaphor for how Jesus came to seek and save those who are lost.

Like Hagar, we are seen by God, loved by God, and cared for by God—even in the midst of the brokenness and the pain. "Where have you come from and where are you going," the Angel of the Lord asked Hagar. Here's the thing. God already knew the answer to both questions, but it was important for Hagar to say where she was on her journey. To admit out loud where she had been, and where she was headed.

Friend, where have you come from? Where are you going? When was the last time you looked—really looked—at your life? Is there something you're running from, or pain that you're allowing to define your path? When the Angel spoke to Hagar, she listened to what God had to say to her. It didn't mean life was suddenly going to be easy, but it did mean God was working, and going before her in all of it. There were parts of her story that she had no control over, and there were parts that she did. At that moment in the desert, Hagar had the chance to pause and choose which path to take. These moments of pause can be life-changing for us, too. What is it that God is calling you to do at this moment in your life?

Take a moment to look back over your life and see how God protected you from something. Think about a time He shone His truth so that you could understand a sin or struggle. Maybe there were some amazing big encounters with Him, but don't forget the little ones, too. He gives us the chance to hear from Him every day. In the messiness and the brokenness of life, in the pain and overwhelming situations, He is there with us. In our own struggles—health, finances, jobs, relationships—we have the chance to cry out to God. He sees us where we are, but He never wants to leave us in the desert. He wants to work in our lives and all of it happens on the backdrop of His mercy and grace.

3. God Speaks Life into the Brokenness

So, what do we do with the fact that we are broken people living in a broken world? The invitation of redemption can be a scary one. God speaks truth into our brokenness and tells us what we need to hear, not necessarily what we want to hear. In those moments, God provides a way for us to move forward by stepping back into the calling and plan He has for us.

Even in the sin-filled situations happening around us, we have the opportunity to reflect truth. We can shine the truth that is found in the Word of God, based on the power of God, that reveals the redemptive plan of God. But it's only going to happen if we have our eyes focused on Jesus because it's so easy to get distracted by the ways of this world and the desires going on inside of us.

This world is hard. Life is hard. It's messy and broken. But let me tell you something, God is not. He's completely put together, He's completely whole. He's completely clean, He's completely loving.

With everything in us, let's run hard after Him! Let's recognize that He is on the throne and let's worship Him through it all. We can see God even from the broken places and broken spaces of life, and He sees us, too. Always remember that:

Trouble does not surprise God. In our overwhelming circumstances, we need to know that God knows what's going on. We can ask him, "Lord, do you have any idea what's going on down here?" But we can know that without exception, His answer is always, "Yes, I see. I know."

Trouble does not overwhelm God. He's not sitting on the throne wondering, "What should I do with the situation? How should I deal with this mess?" He is not in any way undone by the trouble we face!

Trouble does not negate God's plan. In fact, it's often through trouble that God reminds us about His sufficiency as we experience His presence in the brokenness of life. Jesus pulls us into a closer, abiding relationship with Himself through the hard times. *"Jesus said, 'I have told you these things so that in me you may have peace. You will have suffering in this world. Be courageous! I have conquered the world'"* (John 16:33).

4. A Chance to Start Over

It wasn't until Hagar heard from God that she was able to turn around—literally. Thankfully, when we need a reset in our own lives, we don't have to run into the desert first! We don't have to wait for our lives to fall apart before we are open to life change.

The challenge for us is to actively choose healing and sanctification. This may look like stopping a sinful pattern or setting a healthy boundary. It may look like using journaling or therapy to process past trauma or abuse. When we choose to go to God with our brokenness, it gives us a chance for a reset. Journaling, accountability, persistent and intentional prayer—all of those can help on our journey. It's easy to think that all the work is up to God and ourselves, but one of the greatest blessings God gives us in our struggles is community. Surround yourself with close friends who know the nitty-gritty details of your life and struggles. Give these people permission to tell you what you need to hear, not what you want to hear. It takes time for relationships like these to develop, but it is crucial for us to have this accountability!

Once God highlights a struggle, we can look for precepts to follow and promises to claim from the Bible for the area of sin, struggle, pride, or complacency. Once you have a word from the Word, journal about the struggle and God's ongoing sanctifying process. Writing down God's work helps us to process what is going on at a deeper level. It also provides a way for us to go back and see God's ongoing work of sanctification in our life.

Sometimes we're not open to doing the deeper sanctifying work. A lot of times we just want to escape, find an easier situation. We take all the blame or none of the blame. We saw that Sarai looked at God through the lens of her circumstances and blamed Him. Hagar looked at the situation and just walked out on it all. But that wasn't the end of their journeys, and we are not at the end of ours either.

As we surrender to God's plan over our plan, we have the chance to see Him from the middle of our mess and brokenness. Redemption is always on the heart and mind of God. He is the constant in the brokenness. Genesis 16 was hard. It was messy. It was broken. But God was working even in their mess, just like He works in the middle of our mess. Jesus is intimately involved in the challenges going on in our lives, and He is establishing truth and providing a way forward. The question is: Will we follow the One who sees?

Transforming Truth:
God sees, He knows, and He cares.

"Lord, we love You and we desperately need You! We need Your help and we need Your healing. We need Your power and Your truth. More than anything, God, we need a passion to pursue You. We're asking You to do a supernatural work in and through our lives that turns our desert into a spring of living water. Help us to recognize our own brokenness, pain, compromise, and sin. Help us to trust You because we know You see us and love us through it all.

Lord, may our sins make us feel sick instead of excited, chained instead of free, empty instead of complete, and out of control instead of in control.

Lord, prune us. Cut away and remove the distractions, the excess, and the wrong expectations or perspectives.

Lord, shine Your bright light into every dark corner of our souls. Please show us the hidden lies in our lives.

Please show us Your hope, Your redemption plan, the truth, and the peace that You continually offer to anyone who believes. And Lord, we believe. In Jesus' name, amen."

DISCUSSION QUESTIONS

As we journey through the life of Abraham, think about your life. What is God cultivating in you? How can faith and trust grow in your life? What is your greatest struggle? What is defining you in this season of your journey?

Chapter 6: The God Who Sees

1. Like Abram, we live in a broken world. Discuss the culture or world where we live and how it is defined by brokenness and sin.
2. Not only does brokenness define our culture, but it also defines our lives and sometimes our families. Do you or your family face a broken situation that leaves you wondering if God sees you?
3. How can we be swayed by a temporary, worldly mindset that tempts us to try and solve our problems or create purpose and provision in our lives? How does tension in your relationships cause you to run or hide?
4. Share about a time when God met you in your desert and he spoke truth or direction into your broken situation. What does it mean to you to know that God sees you, and that you can experience His work in your life? What would it look like for you to move forward in faith and obedience in the broken areas of life?

This leads to our Transforming Truth: God sees, He knows, and He cares.

5. Discuss the hope the gospel brings to your life and our world. Let's celebrate together that no one is beyond God's reach. (Including you and your family members!) God loves you and He longs to deliver you from your desert running. How do you plan to share the gospel with others as a result of God's redeeming work in you?

Chapter 7

Marked by God

I hope God is meeting you at your point of need as we journey through the life of Abram! Just like Abram, God pursues us intentionally and purposefully and with such a caring and loving heart. I want us to celebrate that truth together. God meets us where we are, He speaks truth into our lives, and He calls us to walk by faith. And, every step of the way, we learn that we can trust Him because He is good and has a good plan. We see that time and time again through the life of Abram.

Yes, Abram blew it at times. Yes, Abram had struggles. Yes, Abram compromised. But God was ever faithful. That's what we're going to see in Genesis 17. A life that trusts God is a life that is marked by God. I can't wait to dig into this part of Abram's story with you!

His Journey

In Genesis 16, we left Abram in a mess with Hagar, Ishmael, and Sarai. Maybe Abram wondered, "Did I blow it? It's been fourteen years since Ishamel was born. Has God given up on me? Will God leave me out of His plan after all?" Abram may have questioned, "Could Ishmael be the child of the promise? Could he be the one that God blessed and honored?" Maybe Abram was just trying to get through life one day at a time, thinking, "How can I deal with all the conflict with Sarai, Hagar, and Ishmael?"

Abram was once again just living his life when God showed up in Genesis 17. God called him to do something very specific, which would mark him and his descendants for the rest of their lives. In the process, Abram would finally get that name change we have been waiting for! So, let's look at Genesis 17, where we will discover four key points, leading to our transforming truth: *Trusting God leads to a life marked by God.*

1. God Set Abram Apart

When Abram was ninety-nine years old, the Lord appeared to him, saying, "I am God Almighty. Live in my presence and be blameless."

Genesis 17:1

Why would God open with this phrase? I assume Abram needed to hear it. Abram had already lived for ninety-nine long years, and God was saying, "Abram, don't forget who I am!" Think about it. Abram was not a spring chicken! He had seen a lot of things in the twenty-four years since his original encounter with God in Genesis 12.

Once again, we see that God appeared to Abram and spoke powerful words. God said, "I am God Almighty." The original name here, translated as 'God Almighty,' is El Shaddai. This name "refers to God's all sufficiency and mighty power to accomplish His promises, according to His will and timeline." [28] This is the first time the name 'El Shaddai' was used in the Bible and I love that. First times were always important because it meant God was revealing more of Himself and His plan to His people. God was doing something new in Abram's life and that work was rooted in God's mighty power.

Let's think about the significance of God doing a new thing. The Lord wanted Abram to know and believe that he served the One who was mighty to save. *Knowing who God is and how God faithfully works would center Abram in the ability of God.* Abram needed to know that God was the One who could carry out His plan and in His own timing. Once God established Himself as almighty, He added, "Live in My presence." Let that sink in! God was reminding Abram, *"I'm your safe place. So, know Me. Experience Me. Let My presence be like a home for you."* If Abram accepted God's invitation, Abram would have the chance to move to the heartbeat of God, seeing the things of God, and living out the promises of God.

In Genesis 12, at that first encounter, God established the promise with Abram and told him he'd be the father of many nations. What God was saying this time is, "All the details of the covenant, and of your life—all of that pales in comparison to just you and Me." That is so gripping for Abram's life. All through his journey, he was trying to figure out his future. "When is this son going to come? Who is the son? What will my legacy be?" God was saying, "I'm God and you're not. Just live in My presence, and I'll take care of the rest."

Spending time in God's presence would lead Abram to cultivate the things of God in his life. Abram could learn to respond to his circumstances out of his relationship with God, not out of his own human understanding. That type of mindset was going to be very important in this "new season" God had for Abram. It would be key to victory.

God knew that if Abram put his eyes on the circumstances, Abram would reflect his own feelings or thoughts about his circumstances. But, when Abram lived in God's presence, with his eyes on God, he could reflect God.

At the beginning of Genesis 17, God was reestablishing Himself as the center of Abram's life. God was reminding Abram that He is almighty, sufficient, and able. And in response to that, God was inviting Abram, to live **to** God, **with** God, **for** God, and **through** God.

2. God Changed Abram's Identity

"'I will set up my covenant between me and you, and I will multiply you greatly." Then Abram fell facedown and God spoke with him: "As for me, here is my covenant with you: You will become the father of many nations. Your name will no longer be Abram; your name will be Abraham, for I will make you the father of many nations."
Genesis 17:2-5

We are finally to the new thing God was doing in Abram's life. And friend, when God moves, He moves! In the Old Testament, names often showed the work God was doing in a person's life. By changing Abram's name to Abraham, God showed that He was moving forward with His promise of making Abraham the father of a new nation. A nation that would be God's people. What God was doing would last for generations, but what kicked it off was this name change. Everything had been building up slowly for Abraham, and then it happened quickly. When God says something is ready, all the resources are in place. Everything that God has been orchestrating comes together and it HAPPENS.

The name change was significant because this was a defining moment. It was a spiritual marker, like when God reaffirmed the promise and Abraham built the altar in Genesis 13 and 14. When we look through Abraham's story in Genesis, we see a pattern emerging. Each time God showed up to meet with Abraham, He built on the promise. He made the promise in Genesis 12, and every time since then He had reaffirmed and expanded it.

Abraham's new name would reflect the way God would change his life. Every time Abraham's name was spoken it would serve as a reminder of God's promise. From that day forward, Abraham was going to be known by the promise God made to him—father of a multitude.

God continued the conversation in Genesis 17:6-8 by sharing a series of "I will" statements. These "I will" statements set the stage for Abraham's "Yes, Lord" moment. Listen to what God said to Abraham:

- I WILL make you very fruitful.
- I WILL make nations of you, and kings will come from you.
- I WILL establish My covenant as an everlasting covenant between me and you and your descendants after you for the generations to come, to be your God and the God of your descendants after you. The whole

land of Canaan, where you now reside as a foreigner, I WILL give as an everlasting possession to you and your descendants after you; and I WILL be their God.

We can sort these "I WILL" promises into three basic areas.

- Fruitfulness: "I will make you fruitful. Even nations and kings will come from you."
- Covenant: "I will make a covenant with you and your descendants."
- Land: "I will give you and your descendants the land."

Wow! Talk about promises to get excited about. After years of Abraham waiting and struggling, God reminded Abraham firmly of His faithfulness. It was like God was saying, "Here's what I did, and here's what I'm going to do. Boom, boom, boom. Now we're rolling!" I imagine Abraham took a deep breath at the sheer magnitude of these promises made which would turn into promises kept.

Up until now, it had been a promise from God that Abraham had the chance to respond to. But God was ready to develop that promise into a covenant—a more formalized agreement made with more than one person. And God was about to tell Abraham his part of the covenant. It would require a serious commitment on Abraham's part.

3. God Challenged Abraham

God also said to Abraham, "As for you, you and your offspring after you throughout their generations are to keep my covenant. This is my covenant between me and you and your offspring after you, which you are to keep: Every one of your males must be circumcised.... My covenant will be marked in your flesh as a permanent covenant. If any male is not circumcised in the flesh of his foreskin, that man will be cut off from his people; he has broken my covenant."
Genesis 17:9-14

God was clear. He wanted Abraham and all of his male descendants to be marked by circumcision (surgical removal of the foreskin). Had he heard of circumcision from other nomads? Could he guess how it would affect him, Ishmael, and the rest of his descendants? God was doing something unique with Abraham, and with his descendants to come. By telling them to cut away part of their body that made them resemble the other nations, God was marking His people.

There are historical records of circumcision existing in Egypt and other regions, but not as a way to distinguish an entire nation! God was doing something unique with Abraham, and with his descendants to come. Circumcision would become a sign of obedience for Abraham and the nation of Israel; an outward expression of an inward reality. And, because this command came in the context of a covenant, it would be a visible reminder to them that they were set apart as God's people. If there were questions swirling in Abraham, God cut through them by continuing.

God said to Abraham, "As for your wife Sarai, do not call her Sarai, for Sarah will be her name. I will bless her; indeed, I will give you a son by her. I will bless her, and she will produce nations; kings of peoples will come from her." Genesis 17:15-16

Abraham was not the only one getting a new name. Sarai was also getting one! Sarah had no children and she was beyond childbearing years, but God Almighty was working in her life, too. Even though Abraham had already had a few divine encounters with God, this promise still sounded ridiculous. And he literally laughed at God's plan.

Abraham fell facedown. Then he laughed and said to himself, "Can a child be born to a hundred-year-old man? Can Sarah, a ninety-year-old woman, give birth?" So Abraham said to God, "If only Ishmael were acceptable to you!" Genesis 17:17-18

Abraham stated the obvious: he and Sarah were old. Having a child was laughable. He had his own suggestion: "What if Ishmael could be the child of promise?"

But God said, "No. Your wife Sarah will bear you a son, and you will call him Isaac. I will confirm my covenant with him as a permanent covenant for his future offspring. As for Ishmael, I have heard you. I will certainly bless him.... But I will confirm my covenant with Isaac, whom Sarah will bear to you at this time next year."
Genesis 17:19-21

God's response brought Abraham and Sarah to a crossroads moment. Were they open to following God and His plan? Was Abraham open to God doing miraculous work in and through his life? If so, Abraham would have to be open to God rearranging his life and marking it in a unique way.

4. Abraham Obeyed in the Moment

On that very day Abraham and his son Ishmael were circumcised. And all the men of his household—whether born in his household or purchased from a foreigner—were circumcised with him.
Genesis 17:26-27

"On that very day!" Abraham didn't continue to argue or debate with God. No. He chose to be obedient. Abraham's, "Yes, Lord," impacted his actions and showed the work that God was doing in his life. Abraham, Ishmael, and every male in his family—all of them were circumcised. I can't imagine the confusion among Abraham's people on that day! They may have been wondering, "Has Abraham lost his mind?" But God knew the importance of the circumcision process for Abraham and his descendants (and there would be a lot of them). *God knew that they needed an outward sign reminding them of the inward reality that they belonged to God Almighty. They needed a reminder that every day they had the chance to live in His presence.*

That's the beauty of being marked by God. Abraham was chosen and set apart by God. In turn, God was inviting Abraham to trust Him. Abraham's trust in God led him to actions that were obedient to God's plan. The best part—God was in the middle of it all!

Obviously, in Genesis 17, there were a lot of outward changes. God changed Abram to Abraham. God changed Sarai to Sarah. God gave an outward sign of the covenant which was circumcision. All of these outward changes represented an inward reality that Abraham and his people belonged to God. Daily we have the chance for our lives to be marked by God in powerful and personal ways.

Our Journey

When I was a little girl, I learned about tithing. On the drive to church every Sunday morning, my parents gave me and my siblings each an envelope for us to add our dollar for the offering. Printed on my envelope were checkboxes for goals, like "I went to church" or "I went to outreach night." Obviously we wanted to check all those boxes because it would be celebrated when we got to our children's classes! Eventually, I started to believe that "checking boxes" was what obedience was—doing all the good things and checking all the boxes, literally.

As I grew older, I kept looking at the good things I did on the outside to see if I was good enough. But as God worked on me, I saw how backwards that was. Those goals and activities were good things, but the best thing—my friendship with Jesus—was really what counted! I still love checking off boxes, but these days I check in with God to see if my heart is right with Him. That is way more important than checking whether I have enough boxes marked off.

-Andrea

Genesis 17 highlights what a life marked by God looks like—change from the inside out. Being marked by God changes us when we show up to life every single day. It helps us say "yes" to Him and "no" to ourselves as we react to how He's leading and guiding us. It reminds us that He is God and we are not. It reminds us that every single day we have the privilege to be a part of God's purpose and plan. Then our obedience becomes an outward sign reminding us of an inward reality.

We are the people of God. We are marked with the righteousness of Jesus Christ. And because of that, we can walk in obedience, which becomes the outward expression of our relationship with God. Obedience opens the door for us to see and experience more of His plans and purposes. And God's plan is never static; it's constantly unfolding and challenging us. God is writing a story that we follow one step at a time, just like Abraham. When we come to 'impossible' roadblocks, God's not worried, because He already knows what's coming. It's like God is saying, "This is going to happen in a way that you never dreamed possible. It's not going to fit your line of thinking. It's not even possible outside of Me!"

If we remind ourselves that we belong to God, our actions flow from our hearts, not from some list of rules. This is especially important for people who grew up in the church. Many people (including believers!) think that religion is just made up of outward things like how we act, or what 'spiritual' boxes we check. And friend, there's a place for all of that! Of course, we want our actions to line up with God and His perfect Word. *But, obedience doesn't start with the outside action, it starts with the inward condition of the heart.* The inward change then results in an outward change—beautiful!!

1. God Sets Us Apart

Faith sometimes looked different in the Old Testament and the New Testament, but the core of what God was doing has always been the same. Faith has always been God's economy. In Hebrews 11, we learn that it was Abraham and Sarah's faith that ultimately led to what God did in and through their lives. It has always been the same God and the same call for God's children to walk by faith. Sometimes the details just look different.

God's work always leads to a life that reflects God's glory, and that is connected to God's purpose and plan. In the Old Testament, circumcision was a visible way that God's people chose to be set apart. In our day, we have a less visible way—we place our faith in Jesus so His righteousness becomes our righteousness. Then, as the Holy Spirit lives in us, we are able to show the difference Jesus makes in us. This leads to outward steps of obedience like baptism.

Abraham was called to live in God's presence and be blameless, and so are we. The call to be blameless is grounded in the holiness of God. In the middle of your challenging circumstance, in the middle of your overwhelming situation, in the middle of your waiting season: God has a plan for you. It's for you to be holy, just as He is holy (1 Peter 1:16). Friend, that can be so hard because we live in a sinful world, and our flesh is sinful. We often want to give in and compromise. Choosing to have a pure heart is much harder!

We may be overwhelmed by God calling us to do or be something. It may be a monumental plan that impacts others. But at the end of the day, we just get to live in the presence of God. And the Holy Spirit is living inside us to help us on our way. In this chapter, God was saying to Abraham, "You get both. You get Me and the legacy, too. You get it all! But before we get to that, remember who I am. I am God almighty, and You get to live in my presence." It's that nugget of truth that simplifies life for us.

We have to be careful about drawing conclusions based on our temporary perspective. It's easy to think, "Genesis 17 means God will give me whatever I want. A big house. A child. Healing from my sickness or healing in my marriage." But we can't bring our wishlist to the table and say we get it all. What Abraham got from God was specifically for God's glory. The application here is not that we get it all. The application here is that daily we get to practice the presence of God because He is God almighty and we are invited to live in His presence. This invitation means we can enjoy ongoing communication with God, doing what He's telling us to do.

Beginning the day with Jesus is fantastic, but time with Him isn't supposed to be just a compartmentalized beginning to our day. It's a springboard to the WHOLE day. Starting out with Jesus sets the tone for communication with Him throughout the rest of our day. What we look at, we reflect. When we gaze at Jesus, we see Jesus for who He is, and God's power shines through us.

2. God Changes Our Identity

When we think about our lives and our realities, we have a limited vision, but God sees us through the righteousness of Christ. When God looks at you, He sees you as redeemed, freed, forgiven, holy, loved, and chosen. When He looks at you, He sees a child who is valued, a child who is adopted. From condemned to saved, from lost to found! As that truth settles into your heart, do you know what happens? It becomes easier to commit to God. That's the beauty of a relationship. When we are in relationship with God, we want to do the things that bring Him glory, that honor Him, and that reflect His work in and through our lives. And God is calling us deeper still, into sustainable, deep commitment that flows from a heart that pursues Jesus and invites Him to change the way we live.

Maybe you're in a strong and fulfilling season of life, where God feels close, your faith seems strong, and your community is loving and supportive. Or maybe you've given up on God, on yourself, or on your faith community. Whatever your season, God has not given up on you! Even today, He gives you the chance to 'reset' and be marked by God.

When we look through the Bible, we see God 'resetting' His people over and over again. From Joshua and the growing tribes to Jesus' headstrong disciples, redemption is God's heart for His people. Taken out of its historical context, the Old Testament can seem harsh. But it's not! It was God carving out a people for Himself, in unique ways, and we see that in His covenants with them. Whether He was making a covenant with Noah, Abraham, or Moses, it showed how much God wanted to have a relationship with His creation, and how human sin had to be dealt with for that to happen. When reading the Old Testament, it makes so much more sense if we understand that God was building a chosen family, people, and nation. Everything He did for them was intentional, as He built their identity. Can we believe the same for ourselves?

3. God Challenges Us

In just this one section of Genesis, we see Abraham deal with two challenges from God. Not only were he and his household (possibly including those 300 fighting men) called to undergo the surgery of circumcision, but God also told him that Sarah would have a baby.

God's plan didn't make sense from a human perspective. I mean, Abraham laughed in his heart, just thinking about Sarah having a child. At 90, Sarah's womb was obviously beyond child-bearing years. Yet, God was going to bring life from that womb. What a picture of the very thing God does for us, bringing spiritual life where there is no life! In the New Testament, Jesus came out of that tomb—alive! The heart of the Christian message has always been death to life!

When it came to circumcision, I don't imagine it was easy for Abraham to convince the other men in his household that they needed to undergo it. In the same way, it's not easy to convince ourselves that we need to leave behind old habits or sins to follow God more fully. In Romans 2:28-29, Paul refers to circumcision when trying to explain what following Jesus looks like.

> *For a person is not a Jew who is one outwardly, and true circumcision is not something visible in the flesh. On the contrary, a person is a Jew who is one inwardly, and circumcision is of the heart—by the Spirit, not the letter.*
> Romans 2:28-29

God has the big picture safe in His heart. He knows the story, He has a plan, and we can trust him. But we have to be open to God rearranging our lives and our legacies. Sometimes the way we would write our story doesn't line up with the way God writes our story. We may try to 'backdoor' God, coming up with an idea that we think God should use in His plan. (As though we can suggest anything new to God!) When we feel

God leading us to something, we might try to negotiate, and make God bless our plans instead. In Abraham's case, it looked like suggesting that Ishmael could be the child of the promise, since no other miracle baby had arrived via Sarah. For us, that might look like suggesting God could hurry up on giving us a spouse, a career, or a child as well. If His promises seem too vague, we may bring up 'solutions' that make sense to us. But let's look at some of the promises He gave us throughout the Bible for us. God made these "I will" statements and we can claim them over our lives:

I will be with you.

I will make a way for you.

I will never leave you nor forsake you.

When God challenges us by asking us to take a step of faith or obedience, these "I will" statements should be firmly rooted in our lives. This will keep us from saying, "God, I will listen to what you say...and then I will do what I think is best." Instead, we will say, "God, You made 'I will' statements over my life. I will trust your way over my way. I will say yes to your storyline for my life!"

4. We Obey in the Moment

For Abraham, being obedient looked like circumcision. For us, it's going to look different. It may be taking a meal to somebody in need. It may be sharing the gospel with someone who doesn't know Jesus. It may be helping somebody in a parking lot, or inviting someone to church. Or keeping our mouth shut in a challenging situation and trusting God to take care of that situation. It may be giving a circumstance or something to God and saying, "I don't know what to do with this, but I trust that You do." Here is an important question to consider: "What does obedience look like for you in this season of life?"

When we think about our mess-ups and struggles, we may also wonder, "Is God still faithful to me?" Like Abraham, we can't see the next chapter in our own story. We have a limited perspective when it comes to what God's doing in the midst of our brokenness and pain. From a human perspective, life is hard, uncertain, and dangerous. But I challenge you to look at life as an exciting faith adventure! Every day we get to wake up and say, "God, you are God and I am not!" Every day we get to wake up and say, "Lord, here am I, send me!" Every day we get to wake up and live **to** God, **with** God, **for** God, and **through** God. How do we do that? By focusing on inward realities that lead to outward expressions of obedience and faith. God is a promise maker and He is a promise keeper. He calls us into a deeper, trusting relationship with Himself, into remembering that He is willing and able to make a way for us.

Together, we are a community of believers who celebrate and proclaim the promises of God. We serve El Shaddai, God Almighty! Through Jesus, God showed that He's 'all in' with us. And every single day we have the chance to show that we are "all in" with him. We, like Abraham, can put our yes on the table, even before we know the outcome of that yes. That, my friend, is faith and faith changes how we live!

Transforming Truth:
Trusting God leads to a life marked by God.

"Lord, thank You that we can always trust You. We want to be challenged and we want to be changed by You. Help our inward relationship with You lead to outward expressions of faith that reflect your glory. Lord, we know this is our right and our privilege as believers in Jesus Christ. Help us to live what we believe and let that belief flow from a deep and personal walk with El Shaddai, God Almighty! In the powerful name of Jesus, we pray, amen."

DISCUSSION QUESTIONS

As we journey through the life of Abraham, think about your life. What is God cultivating in you? How can faith and trust grow in your life? What is your greatest struggle? What is defining you in this season of your journey?

Chapter 7: Marked by God

1. God introduced Himself as God Almighty or El Shaddai. What does El Shaddai mean to you, especially during challenging seasons? Share about a time when you saw the mightiness of God on display.
2. God changed Abram's name to line up with the plan God had for Abraham's life. If God changed your name to represent His work in your current season of life, what would your name be? How would this name point to a chance to trust God at a deeper level?
3. Abraham had to be open to a move of God in his life and among his family. This move made everyone uncomfortable. Are you open to following God and His plan even if it is uncomfortable? Are you open to God rearranging your life or your family's life?
4. I shared my struggle with basing my level of spirituality on a checklist approach to God. Have you struggled with this tendency in your life? How does this tendency keep us focused on ourselves and our actions rather than on God and His plan?

This leads to our Transforming Truth: Trusting God leads to a life marked by God.

5. Imagine what it would be like to have an attitude of, "God, before I even know what you're asking for, I'm available, because I KNOW WHO YOU ARE. Even if it comes in a package that I don't expect, I'm going to be obedient—I'm going to live your way." Describe how this type of attitude would lead to a life marked by God.

Chapter 8

Little by Little

Abraham and Sarah were on a real-life faith adventure. Sometimes it was messy and other times it was meaningful, just like our own lives. Through it all, God was working. Are you ready to cover lots of ground in Abraham's journey? We are going to cover Genesis 18, 20, and 21. Lots of things happen during this span of time. As we walk through these chapters we are going to see an important concept that God used in the lives of Abraham, the Nation of Israel, and our lives, too. The concept is called **little by little.**

God works—little by little.
God provides—little by little.
God moves—little by little.
God teaches—little by little.

The phrase **little by little** does not lead to small or insignificant results, but big and profound ones. The phrase **little by little** shows the heart of God to work according to His plan in order to accomplish His purpose.

His Journey

God's plan continued to unfold for Abraham and Sarah. Think about how far Abraham and Sarah had come since their first encounters with God in Genesis 12. They were learning how to follow God. They were making progress even if they didn't know it. God was cultivating faith and trust in their journey. It's my prayer that God will continue to cultivate faith and trust in us.

Remember where we left Abraham. He, his son Ishmael, his family, and every male in his possession were circumcised—visibly marked—as a sign of the covenant. The establishment of the covenant led to specific, exciting things happening in Abraham's journey, and everything was happening according to God's timeline. So, let's look at Genesis 18, 20, and 21, where we will explore three separate encounters in Abraham's journey. Along the way, we will discover four key points, leading to our transforming truth: *Trusting God means trusting His timing.*

1. Nothing was Impossible for God

Abraham was at the oaks of Mamre, a name that represented intimacy with God. At the oaks, God showed up and did something beautiful and specific.

The Lord appeared to Abraham at the oaks of Mamre while he was sitting at the entrance of his tent during the heat of the day.
Genesis 18:1

Abraham saw three men standing nearby. We know from the rest of the section that one was God, and it's believed that the other two were angels. Abraham, recognizing the importance of his visitors, bowed down to the ground and asked them to stay for a meal. While there, the Lord told him that in one year, Sarah would give birth to a son. Sarah was in the background listening to the conversation and actually laughed because she knew that she and Abraham were (way) past childbearing years! Both of them were old, and certainly from a human standpoint having a child was no longer possible. The Lord heard Sarah laughing, and had a conversation with Abraham about it.

But the Lord asked Abraham, "Why did Sarah laugh, saying, 'Can I really have a baby when I'm old?' Is anything impossible for the Lord? At the appointed time I will come back to you, and in about a year she will have a son."
Genesis 18:13-14

Sarah was caught laughing at the plan of God. It's easy to see why she laughed. She had waited and longed for this announcement for many years. And once it finally happened, it was 'too late.' (I can just imagine Sarah listening in and laughing at what the Lord said. To have a baby, there had to be some sort of physical union between Sarah and Abraham. Maybe that was even funnier to her than the idea of her being pregnant at 90+ years old.) It was an impossible future—which meant God was going to get all the glory from the birth announcement!

Try reading God's question from verse 13 with an emphasis on God's ability. "Is anything impossible for the Lord?" Abraham and Sarah were going to have to wrestle with this question and answer it with a "yes" or "no." Yes, they believed that nothing was too difficult for the Lord. Or, no they didn't. It was going to bring them to a point of decision. And this was before they knew how God was going to answer, before He reminded them of a promise or opened a door. Our circumstances may point to something being totally impossible, but our circumstances do not determine our God! Our God determines our circumstances.

Now, try reading the question this way: "Is anything impossible for the *Lord*?" I love that this question focused on the Lord. It didn't focus on Abraham or Sarah or their circumstances including their age, or the current reality of their lives. No, the question pointed toward the Lord and His ability. *"Is anything impossible for the Lord?"* In the midst of overwhelming circumstances and situations, the answer to this question reveals what a person truly believes about God.

Of course, we know the end of the story. We know that one year later Abraham and Sarah gave birth to a son. The answer to God's question is that nothing is impossible for Him!

2. *God Invited Abraham In*

The conversation continued between Abraham and the men. Abraham received some pretty shocking news about the place where his nephew Lot lived.

The men got up from there and looked out over Sodom, and Abraham was walking with them to see them off. Then the Lord said, "Should I hide what I am about to do from Abraham? Abraham is to become a great and powerful nation, and all the nations of the earth will be blessed through him. For I have chosen him so that he will command his children and his house after him to keep the way of the Lord by doing what is right and just. This is how the Lord will fulfill to Abraham what he promised him."
Genesis 18:16-19

God invited Abraham into a conversation about what would happen to Sodom. God shared that He was considering wiping out Sodom because of its sin—seen from God's perspective. This led to a conversation between Abraham and the Lord.

Since Lot lived near Sodom, I imagine Abraham's heart was moved when he thought about what would happen to Lot if Sodom was destroyed. Abraham asked a series of questions presenting a case to save the city if fifty righteous people, or even only ten righteous people, were found. The Lord investigated Sodom but found that there were not even ten people who followed God. True to His word, God ended up destroying the city. But the Lord rescued Lot and brought him and his family out.

What I find fascinating is that God wanted Abraham to be involved in what was going on in Abraham's world. The destruction of Sodom was not a light choice for God. God was inviting Abraham to see His will unfold in real-time, and even to have some influence. During the conversation, Abraham grew to see the situation from God's perspective of compassion, but also of pure holiness. I believe that Abraham's questions, and pleading for the lives of people in Sodom, led to Lot being rescued. And when God did destroy the city, Abraham was able to understand what was really going on.

3. God Never Gave Up on Abraham

Let's pick up in Genesis 20. Abraham was in a different place. He was no longer by the great trees of Mamre, which represented intimacy with God. Instead, Abraham was down south in the Negev between Kadesh and Shur. Being in the southern part of the land, with new neighbors and possible threats, must have stirred up some insecurities. Once again, Abraham told a king that Sarah was his sister instead of his wife!

Genesis 20 is so beautiful because we see how, again, God didn't give up on His people. God was faithful every step of the way.

King Abimelech took Sarah into his possession, but God appeared to the king in a vision and told him he needed to give Sarah back to Abraham. Thankfully, the king was a person of integrity. He called in Abraham and asked him, "Why did you trick me?" Something important comes out of the conversation between Abraham and the king.

> *Abraham replied, "I thought, 'There is absolutely no fear of God in this place. They will kill me because of my wife.' Besides, she really is my sister, the daughter of my father though not the daughter of my mother, and she became my wife. So when God had me wander from my father's house, I said to her: Show your loyalty to me wherever we go and say about me, 'He's my brother.'"*
> Genesis 20:11-13

This confession by Abraham is important for us to understand. Especially as the birth of Isaac was close to fulfillment. God had Abraham look at an earlier sin that had been plaguing his entire journey. Apparently when God told Abraham to leave his home country and go to the land God would show him, Abraham and Sarah had a conversation that went something like this. "Hey, Sarah, this is how you can prove that you love me. You can say you're my sister instead of my wife. Which is not TECHNICALLY a lie.... If we're ever in a dangerous situation, we'll just use this excuse to save ourselves and buy some time." Now we understand why Abraham asked Sarah to lie on multiple occasions!

The very future promised to Abraham and Sarah was being filtered through their unbelief. God had promised to make Abraham and Sarah into a great nation. He was going to provide a descendent through their union as husband and wife. That was the deal; that was the promise. So, it helps clarify the story when we see that they had a long-term, fear-based agreement that did not line up with God's ultimate purpose for them as a family. When we peel back the layers of this statement, we discover Abraham's ongoing struggle to trust God for his life and legacy.

So right before Isaac was born, God brought the issue of unbelief to the surface. Basically, He said, "Abraham, we are going to deal with this one final time." Even though no one else may have known about Abraham's smoldering wrong belief, it led to consequences for others around him. God shut the wombs of the women in the land where Abraham and Sarah lied about their relationship. As a result, Abraham had to pray to God and ask God to open the wombs of the women in the land (Genesis 20:17-18). Don't think for a second that the prayer was lost on Abraham! Abraham had to pray for other people's wombs to be open because he didn't trust God with his wife and her womb. I'd love to talk to Abraham someday in heaven. "When God told you to pray for those wombs to be open...just talk me through that! What were you thinking? How did that prayer change you?" I just can't get over the goodness of God to get Abraham to a place of clarity about his sin and unbelief before Isaac was born.

4. God Fulfilled the Promise

Let's move on to Genesis 21 and I hope you are on the edge of your seat because something big is about to happen. May we never forget that God moves according to His purpose and plan!

The Lord came to Sarah as he had said, and the Lord did for Sarah what he had promised. Sarah became pregnant and bore a son to Abraham in his old age, at the appointed time God had told him.
Genesis 21:1-2

The Lord came and the Lord provided! Finally, after all this time, Sarah gave birth to a son! Can you imagine the joy and relief? The birth of Isaac happened at the very time God promised. Not a day early and not a day late. *God is always on time according to His purpose and plan.*

For just a moment, let's take in the journey. For Abraham and Sarah, it was a long journey from Genesis 12 to Genesis 21. It had been one step forward and two steps back. There were lots of ups and downs, and twists and turns. But God was present and faithful. Abraham and Sarah stayed in the fight, friend. They may have gotten discouraged, and they made wrong choices, but they didn't give up and go back to Ur. Little by little, God provided, and little by little they responded in obedience and faith. And we see this milestone on their journey right here in Genesis 21.

God showed up. God provided just like He said He would. But He did it in His timing, for His reasons.

Isaac's birth led the way for descendants who formed a nation and would inhabit the Promised Land, but their journey was no easier than Abraham's. In Exodus 23:30 and Deuteronomy 7:22, we find that God planned to give them the land 'little by little.' Instead of just immediately bringing them in, He was teaching the nation how to live. He was growing them. He was challenging them. He was transforming them. It was on the landscape of their journey to the Promised Land—that happened little by little— that the nation learned how to rightly possess the land. Let's not forget that the nation had its fair share of ups and downs and mess-ups along the way!

Back in Genesis 11, when God showed up in Abraham's life with amazing promises, He could have made those promises come true immediately, right? But no. God waited and He taught, and He worked and He moved. He provided little by little. And in the process of that, Abraham was changed. He was transformed. He had the chance to show his faith, and he also had a chance to deal with his sin. One thing we see time and time again in Abraham and Sarah's journey is that God was always moving and working. He was changing and transforming. Ultimately, God was shaping Abraham and Sarah to live according to His way, and it happened little by little.

Our Journey

Andrea's Journey

It was just one of those questioning days. "God, does anything I'm doing really matter? Am I even making a difference?" Then a friend texted me unexpectedly. "I just feel like I need to pray for you today. How can I pray?" I wrote back that I was discouraged, even though I knew better. Later that afternoon, I received a text from a second friend, asking how she could pray for me. I thought, "OK, God, You have my attention." I texted the first friend to share, and she wrote back, "I love it because this morning, Andrea, I prayed that God would send somebody to encourage you!"

It made me smile to see how God is faithful to not give up on His people, even on days when we give up on ourselves.   -Andrea

What Abraham believed in his challenging moments, and what God had formed in him in those moments—that was his little by little. What is ours? What does little by little mean for our journey? As we look at Genesis 18, 20, and 21, I want to encourage you to know that God is working little by little in your life. too. God is always doing more than we know. His timeline is never late. We can trust Him.

1. Nothing is Impossible for God

Friend, the ups and downs in your journey do not take God by surprise. He is always in control, and He is always on His throne. Nothing is too hard for the Lord! Little by little, God is working in your life. So, stay in the process. Don't get discouraged. Keep on keeping on. When you have a rough day, reach out to a friend and ask them to pray for you. It can make such a difference in your day and it will help you refocus on God's purpose and plan as revealed little by little in your life.

If even asking someone to pray for you is a challenge, think about why that is. Is it because you don't actually think God can or will help you? Is it because you think God can do things for others— wants to do things for others—but not for you? If so, that ties into so many wrong beliefs you may have, like that you have to earn your way, or be good enough. When we dig down into what we actually believe about God, it can be uncomfortable, but paves the way for unexpected growth.

So often we want God to fix something, we want Him to provide something, or we want Him to change something. Or maybe we want Him to do something new and exciting in our lives. In the midst of our hard and overwhelming times, often we want to give up or quit. We struggle to walk through the challenging season! But as God takes us through it, little by little, we're changed...we're transformed a little more into the image of Jesus Christ. And, as much as we may mess up, God also uses us to reflect His love and plan to others along the way. So when you're in a situation you wish God would hurry up and resolve, remember God is working little by little. And just like the question Abraham and Sarah faced, *"Is anything impossible for the Lord?"* We have to answer the same question in our lives.

2. God Invites Us In

In Genesis 18, we saw God drawing Abraham into what He was doing with Sodom and Gomorrah. It wasn't a one-sided information briefing from God or a one-sided demand from Abraham. It was a time of Abraham talking with God and listening to His reply. Abraham heard what God was planning, and then presented a case on behalf of these cities, because of his nephew. In the process of that conversation, God was also inviting Abraham to see the cities for what they were.

This is something that's important for us too. In our perspective of God's work in our fallen world, we're invited in through prayer, but as we see the plan unfold, we are reminded that God knows what's right. Talking to God and hearing from God protects us from wrongly assessing God's work or motives. The opportunity to connect our hearts with

God's heart serves as a protection for us in a difficult situation.

I imagine that Abraham walked away from that encounter with a sense that the holiness of God had to be taken into account. What was happening in those cities was just so wrong that God had to take action. Sometimes we wonder, "How can a loving God allow this?" Sometimes it's hard to grasp what holiness looks like in a fallen world, and how He can choose to act—or not act—in a way that makes no sense to us. We can argue with Him, or just land at His feet, knowing that He is right and He is good. When we pray, which is communication with God, we are talking to God by sharing our thoughts and we're listening to God for His reply. When there's an abiding relationship, we begin to see things through God's perspective instead of our own. God wants to invite us in, just like He invited Abraham in.

When we think about hard things that are happening in life, we need to talk to God about them. We need to engage in communication and conversation. Bold prayers protect our hearts and minds from misunderstanding who God is and what God is doing. Or maybe mis-processing or mis-assigning blame or guilt when God is doing something different than what we expected. So if you are in a hard situation, I encourage you to communicate with God by both talking and listening. You can ask God to shape your understanding of the situation. Like Abraham, you are a person of influence. You are a believer in Jesus Christ and a person of great value. God wants you to understand that He is good and that His ways are good. And, what God is doing in and through your life and the lives of your loved ones matters for eternity. So let's talk to God about the hard things. Let's run to Him, not from Him.

3. God Never Gives Up on Us

It would have been easy for God to criticize Abraham, or abandon him until Abraham (finally) started making better choices on his own. Instead, God took the time to walk with Abraham through those struggles and bad choices. And He wants to do the same for us.

What we see in the Bible, over and over again, is that God never gives up on His people. He is faithful to show up to meet with them, and He is faithful to correct them. Think of David and Bathsheba, Adam and Eve hiding in the garden, and Jonah running away from God. Think of Peter, Saul-who-became-Paul, and the disciple Thomas. All of them believed lies that didn't line up with God's truth, and God didn't allow those lies to fester. As much as we may want to focus on a convenient or comfortable life, God wants to focus on giving us an abundant life (John 10:10). And that means He is going to help us deal with our sins, anything getting in the way of a fuller life for us, and anything getting in the way of a better relationship with Him. He will invite His people to peel the onion, get to the heart of the sin, and then experience transformation.

Remember we discussed how Abraham fell into the trap again of protecting himself by lying about his relationship with Sarah? That's when we found out that there was a faulty belief Abraham had from the moment they left Haran way back in Genesis 11, and it was still affecting him in Genesis 20. Sometimes we think of correction as being a one-time situation, but in this case, we see God dealing with Abraham's worry and fear throughout the years, and correcting him along the way. He does the same for us, if we're willing to take the time to listen and make the effort to change.

It's important to not skip that oh-so-important process of sanctification. No quick fix can replace us taking the time to dig deep into our own hearts, figuring out the lies we believe, and then engaging in the transformation process. It takes effort to trace those lies of the enemy and of the flesh and replace them with the truth found in God's Word. But the truth sets us free, and is worth all the hard work!

4. God Fulfills the Promise

Do you believe that God is willing and able to move according to His purpose and plan in your life? I hope so because God is faithful to show up, and fulfill His purpose and plan in and through you. Abraham didn't disqualify himself, Sarah didn't disqualify herself. You didn't disqualify yourself, I haven't disqualified myself. But as we surrender and submit to God's timing, His 'little-by-little' timing, His purpose and plan will happen.

In the last section, we thought about people in the Bible who messed up, but whose stories didn't end there. David sinned, but as God dealt with his sin he was able to write psalms of repentance and redemption that still encourage us today. Adam and Eve had to leave the Garden of Eden, but God took care of them as they left. Because Jonah repented and went to Nineveh after all, a whole city of 'pagan' Assyrians turned to God and their city was saved. Jesus had breakfast with Peter on the beach and charged him to help shepherd the new church. Jesus spoke personally to the disciple Thomas and invited him to literally touch His pierced side. And God turned persecutor Saul into the Apostle Paul, who planted churches throughout two continents and wrote large parts of our New Testament. God had a redemptive plan for every single one of those people, with all their doubts and sins.

What about you and me? What can be said about our lives? Especially in the spots where we want God to "change it," "fix it," or "provide it?" Can we commit to God's plan and purpose as little by little we see how:

- God is glorified and I am encouraged and transformed.
- God's Name is spread as I display the difference God makes in me and through me.

These two statements are the full, free abundant life Jesus provides for you and me. It's easy to give lip service to the idea that God will work everything out...but we still want Him to work it out in our timing. At our pace. When we can't see what God is doing, we want Him to fulfill the promise according to our plan and answer all the questions along the way. But through it all, we have the chance—like Abraham—to surrender to God's little-by-little process in our lives knowing that God is glorified and we are encouraged. God's name is spread as we display the difference He makes in and through us. And all of it happens as we trust His timing, not our own.

Transforming Truth:
Trusting God means trusting His timing.

"Lord, we love You and we thank You for Your work in our lives. We thank You for the way You worked little by little in Abraham's life. We thank You for how You've worked little by little in our lives, even in the overwhelming situations where we wish it didn't have to be 'this way.' God, please build our faith to see how You are going to take our challenge and turn it around for Your glory and our good.

Thank You, Lord, that You are always moving according to Your plan and purposes. We praise You, Father, knowing that You hang onto us even when we tend to let go. I ask that You plant the truths we are learning deep in our hearts and minds. Help us to embrace the truth and then live out the truth. I ask You to silence the lies of the enemy in our minds and to empower us to trust You more and more. Lord, we want to see Your plans and purposes come to pass, in Jesus' name, amen."

DISCUSSION QUESTIONS

As we journey through the life of Abraham, think about your life. What is God cultivating in you? How can faith and trust grow in your life? What is your greatest struggle? What is defining you in this season of your journey?

Chapter 8: Little by Little

1. Describe the phrase or concept "little by little." Looking back over your life, share a season or area of life that is described by the little-by-little concept.
2. How have you grown in your faith and trust in God as a result of waiting on God and His timing?
3. Sarah laughed at God. The thought of having a son seemed impossible even though Sarah had been waiting for a son for years. Which part of Sarah's story impacts you and why? How has the impossible been made possible in your life?
4. Abraham revealed the lie of the enemy and of the flesh that he believed from the beginning of his journey. How do lies surface in our lives and cause us to veer from God's plan? God shut the wombs of women as a result of Abraham lying about his relationship with Sarah. How has God used consequences in your life to get you back on track?

This leads to our Transforming Truth: Trusting God means trusting His timing.

5. Daily we have the chance to surrender to God and His 'little-by-little' process in our lives. Describe how God is glorified, you are encouraged, God's name is being spread, and you display the difference God makes in your life as you trust God and His timing, not our own.

Chapter 9

Grace in the Moment

As we come to this final chapter, I'm a little bit emotional. I'm overwhelmed by the goodness of God. I am overwhelmed by the leading of God in our journey. And how everything that He does is for our good and His glory.

Every step of the way God saw Abraham. God placed a call on Abraham's life. God led the way and even when Abraham gave up on the promise, God never gave up on him. I wonder if that truth speaks to you? Do you need to be reminded that God sees you, knows you, and loves you? He has a plan for your life; He has not given up on you!

If I asked you to tell me one thing that happened in Abraham's life, probably the events recorded in Genesis 22 would come to mind. The moment when God tested Abraham by asking him to take Isaac and sacrifice him. We're going to see how the story unfolds and we are going to see the heart of God in the middle of it all. The four key points and transforming truth from Genesis 22 will challenge us if we let them.... That's the beautiful thing about the Word of God; it meets us right where we are and speaks truth into our lives.

His Journey

As we come to this passage, I wish I could interject myself into Abraham and Sarah's story. I would tell them to hang on because God was going to provide in such a miraculous way. At this point in the story, I think of Abraham as being seasoned, wise, and tested. He was more than a hundred years old and had been through a lot. And yet there was still a lot for him to go through. God was about to show His tenderness and provision for Abraham through what was probably the hardest moment in Abraham's journey.

So, let's pick up the story in Genesis 22 and see how the details unfold. We will discover four key points, leading to our transforming truth: *Trusting God leads to grace in the moment.*

1. How Big Was Abraham's Faith?

Time passed between Genesis 21 and Genesis 22. Tension rose between Ishmael and Isaac. Sarah encouraged Abraham to send Hagar and Ishmael away. The decision was hard for Abraham. He loved Ishmael and wanted the best for his son. God promised to provide for Ishmael. So Abraham agreed to send Hagar and Ishmael away.

A new season of life started for Abraham, Sarah, and Isaac. There were some good, normal years for this family of three. I hope, with less fighting at home, and no more big wars between neighboring kings, Isaac grew up and became a young man, learning about the One True God. I imagine the family stories were told, including the promises made and promises kept; the covenants formed and formalized. I bet the stories were celebrated, and there was Isaac, taking it all in. Maybe Sarah and Abraham started hoping for grandchildren, and a peaceful 'retirement' in their old age. Then we read about the events recorded in Genesis 22.

After these things God tested Abraham and said to him, "Abraham!" "Here I am," he answered. "Take your son," he said, "your only son Isaac, whom you love, go to the land of Moriah, and offer him there as a burnt offering on one of the mountains I will tell you about."
Genesis 22:1-2

God showed up and called Abraham by name. God told Abraham to take Isaac, the one he loved, and offer him as a sacrifice. Immediately we think, "Hang on, why would God test Abraham at this point in the journey?"

The Hebrew word for "test" is Nasah. This word means to try or to prove, and carries the idea of refinement.[29] God was refining, proving, testing, and trying Abraham's faith. Why? *Because a refined faith is an obedient faith!*

A refined faith says, "Yes Lord," even before all the details are known. It's a life that is lived **to** God, **with** God, **for** God, and **through** God. The heart of God was not to hurt Abraham or Isaac or Sarah. God was not trying to trip Abraham up or nullify the promise. Rather God was going to show Abraham how much his faith had grown! God was going to show him, "Look, Abraham, your faith is real! Look, Abraham, we've been on this journey together and you have been changed, you have been transformed! You do trust me and you are willing to respond in obedience and faith."

The outcome of Genesis 22 was never in question in God's heart or mind. He knew what was going to happen. God knew what He was going to do. The testing process was important. Through the testing process, Abraham's faith grew stronger. He moved away from his emotions, fears, and human logic. His beliefs and choices started to line up with God's promises and show the work God had been doing in and through his life, all along the way.

Think about where Abraham was in Genesis 12. Worried, doubtful, lying, and scared. Overwhelmed, maybe even surprised by God talking to him. Now in Genesis 22, it's years, maybe decades later. Abraham had to go from a situation of thinking having a child was not possible, to a situation where he had the child but he was being asked to sacrifice him, to a situation where Abraham believed God was able to raise that child from the dead! A lot had to happen in Abraham's heart to get him to trust God at that level.

Abraham surrendered to God because he believed that, no matter what happened to Isaac on that mountain, they were both coming down. He could obey because he believed that promises made would be promises kept. The promise Abraham believed was that Isaac would live, have children, and make Abraham the father of nations. Part of Abraham's promise was external—land and descendants—but part of it was also internal—God would be his shield and reward and nothing was impossible for God.

2. Abraham Worshiped in the Moment

What was Abraham going to do with this test in his life? Was he going to run from it or remain in it? If he remained, how would he get through this season? These are just a few of the questions in my mind as I think about what it was like to face this test.

So Abraham got up early in the morning, saddled his donkey, and took with him two of his young men and his son Isaac. He split wood for a burnt offering and set out to go to the place God had told him about. On the third day Abraham looked up and saw the place in the distance. Then Abraham said to his young men, "Stay here with the donkey. The boy and I will go over there to worship; then we'll come back to you."
Genesis 22:3-5

Can you imagine that moment in Abraham's life? Abraham loved Isaac. Let's not forget the path to having Isaac had been long and hard. Yet, when God called, Abraham got up early the next morning and set out to the place God would show him. Abraham knew what they were going there to do when they arrived at "the place." The intent was to sacrifice Isaac. Abraham obeyed. He responded in obedience to the test of God.

He took servants with him. His servants only went part of the way. Abraham and Isaac had to go all the way.

Did you notice what Abraham said to his servants? He said, *"Stay here with the donkey. The boy and I will go over there to worship; then we'll come back to you."* Talk about faith. Abraham knew that even if he had to sacrifice Isaac, God was able to bring Isaac back from the dead.

Here is where we can see the obedience, belief, and trust that changed the direction of Abraham's life. *God's character, ability, strength, and truth were there for Abraham in the midst of his hard situation. This allowed Abraham to have confidence in God at that moment.* And that helped him walk up that mountain.

What did Abraham call what was going to happen on the mountain? He didn't call it the hardest moment of his life. *He called it worship!* The Hebrew word for worship used in this passage means "to prostrate oneself," or literally lying face down on the ground in respect. It means submission, surrendering to someone more important or powerful.[30] What did worship do for Abraham? It provided the right perspective, seeing God as God. Abraham knew that no matter what happened on the mountain, God was going to take care of it. Somehow he knew that he and Isaac were coming back down the mountain.

3. Abraham Walked Up that Mountain

Yet, Abraham had to put one foot in front of the next and walk up that mountain. *Hard is hard even when it's right.* Abraham was trusting God to work out the situation, but that didn't make the situation easy. Imagine walking up the mountain knowing what was about to happen. Even with faith, that walk was hard.

Abraham took the wood for the burnt offering and laid it on his son Isaac. In his hand he took the fire and the knife, and the two of them walked on together. Then Isaac spoke to his father Abraham and said, "My father." And he replied, "Here I am, my son." Isaac said, "The fire and the wood are here, but where is the lamb for the burnt offering?" Abraham answered, "God himself will provide the lamb for the burnt offering, my son." Then the two of them walked on together.
Genesis 22:6-8

Isaac was taking in every detail. He was looking around and observing the situation."We've got the wood, we've got the fire, but where is the lamb?" Think about that question for Abraham. Even though he trusted God and believed, it had to be a gut-wrenching moment. In his mind, Abraham may have been thinking, "Are we really going to do this?"

Is this really going to happen?" Yet, Abraham continued.

It is important to remember that Isaac was a real person. When the story took place, he was older. We may picture a cute little boy who was unaware of what was happening. But Isaac was a young man. He was someone who knew what it meant to sacrifice to the Lord. He was someone who knew the processes. He knew the steps and that's why he asked the question. To think about what was going on in Isaac's mind is sobering. Isaac had been cared for his whole life. He had been specifically pampered, loved, and protected because of the journey that Abraham and Sarah took in order to have him. I'm sure his mind was racing with all the questions. But he trusted his father. Isaac followed his father into the unusual, uncomfortable, and unknown place. There's a lesson for us in that.

When they arrived at the place that God had told him about, Abraham built the altar there and arranged the wood. He bound his son Isaac and placed him on the altar on top of the wood. Then Abraham reached out and took the knife to slaughter his son. But the angel of the Lord called to him from heaven and said, "Abraham, Abraham!" He replied, "Here I am." Then he said, "Do not lay a hand on the boy or do anything to him. For now I know that you fear God, since you have not withheld your only son from me."
Genesis 22:9-12

Let the scene sink in. Abraham had to take Isaac and bind him up. Abraham had to lay Isaac on the altar. Abraham had to raise his knife. It was at that moment that the angel of the Lord stopped him. Abraham showed complete obedience. Here is the important point. God never intended for Abraham to sacrifice Isaac. God always had another plan.

4. God Provided the Ram

The Angel stopped Abraham, but what would happen next?

Abraham looked up and saw a ram caught in the thicket by its horns. So Abraham went and took the ram and offered it as a burnt offering in place of his son. And Abraham named that place The Lord Will Provide, so today it is said, "It will be provided on the Lord's mountain."
Genesis 22:13-14

Can you imagine the relief Abraham experienced on that mountain? In that nail-biting moment, God sent a ram for Abraham and Isaac. Abraham's test led to a breakthrough moment. ***The Lord will provide!*** That truth was etched in Abraham's soul. All the years of wondering and waiting, led to a resounding moment of faith. One thing Abraham knew for sure—God provides on the mountain.

Friend, God provided the ram. But a day was coming when God would provide a lamb, and we can't miss this important parallel. It's believed that the place where Abraham was willing to sacrifice Isaac was very near the place where Jesus sacrificed His life on our behalf. God always paints a picture of His provision, mercy, and grace. In Abraham's hardest moment, God showed up and He provided a ram. A day was coming when God would provide Jesus, who is the Lamb of God who takes away the sins of the world (John 8:56).

Besides being a huge milestone in Abraham's life, that moment also points to our Savior. God was setting the stage for redemption. All the way back in Genesis 22, as Abraham walked up that mountain, God was painting a picture of the gospel. Jesus, the Lamb of God, would become human, live a sinless life, and walk up a hill to die in our place. We know the rest of the story. Jesus changed the course of human history and made the way for us to be in a relationship with God. Jesus is the way, the truth, and the life (John 14:6)!

In the Bible, we see story after story of redemption and moments when someone could choose to trust God—or not. *Abraham chose to trust God. Isaac chose to trust Abraham. We can choose to trust Jesus.* Ultimately, God showed up at every single point of need, and provided in His own way. He always has and He always will!

Our Journey

When I was a young mom with little boys, I would rock my babies to sleep. Often as I rocked them, I would think about the story of Abraham and Isaac on the mountain. "God, I could never do something so drastic—not that He would ever call any of us to do that!" But, what if He called me to trust Him through an unknown or hard situation with my boys? I did not want to sign up for that! I was young. I was emotional. I remember rocking my babies and secretly hoping God would never ask me to lay them down. I didn't want to have to trust God at that level. I didn't want to put my boys on the 'altar of surrender.' Today, I can say I was so wrong to process the story in that way. Here's why I was so wrong: I came at the story from the perspective of what could have happened, instead of what actually did happen.

-Andrea

Maybe you're like me, and you've looked at this story and thought a million times, "I hope that never happens to me!" But what if we embrace a different perspective? What if we say, *"If and when the test comes, I will remember who God is and how God works."* God is the same yesterday, today, and forever, and we can trust him!

The way we process the story shows our level of trust in God. It hints at our understanding of what our time on earth is really all about. Instead of looking at the story from our human perspective, what if we look at the story from God's perspective? God knew He would be faithful, no matter the circumstance. God knew He would show up—then and always. Maybe not in the way we expect, but God will always provide. At that moment, I believe grace was lavished all over Abraham's life. I imagine him having a literal mountaintop experience: he had believed God, he had trusted God, and God showed up. Abraham would never be the same again.

One thing I have learned over the years is that God is faithful to provide grace in the moment. Maybe you have experienced grace in a hard
season, in a moment when you faced something in God's strength, rather than your own.

I have heard grace described as "God's riches at Christ's expense." God gives us grace during salvation, and grace is always available to us as we meet challenges. The Holy Spirit is working during these moments, helping us choose faith instead of fear. When we trust God, we know that God is with us and God is for us. God is going to provide a way. And His grace fortifies us to meet the hardest of hard, not in our strength but in God's strength.

Maybe you're like me and you've been afraid of what God might want to do in your life. Maybe you're unsure if you can lay your life on His altar. Genesis 22 sets the stage for us to experience freedom, even through doubts or fears. I pray that you will see this passage of Scripture not through the lens of what could have happened but what actually did happen! *The test in your life provides the place for God to show up and provide exactly what you need.*

1. How Big is Our Faith?

Faith is like a muscle. It's not faith until it's used. Proven faith is real faith, because otherwise it's just theoretical. I can say I want to be a woman of faith, but that means nothing until I demonstrate it. It's often through hard times and uncertainties that we see if we really have faith. It's through struggles that we see if we trust God in the midst of it. Refined faith or tested faith leads to obedient faith.

What has God been building in you? You may not see it at the moment, among all of the things that may seem random. But sometimes there's clarity when we step back and look at the big picture journey that was preparing us for this moment.

Just like Abraham, we go through seasons of testing. It's part of our walk with the Lord. We may wonder during our test if we can trust God. If we're not careful, we can think God isn't good or we're in trouble. The test can make us think we did something bad, or we wonder if we can trust God with the outcome. Honestly, the opposite is true. As we learned earlier, the word 'test' used in Genesis 22 carries the idea of refining, and it usually happens during a stressful circumstance. God refines those He loves so they will remain loyal and faithful to Him.

There are times in our walk with God when we will be tested, but God always provides a way. Just like He provided in Abraham's situation, He will provide in our situation. God is not going to put us into a situation of testing and then leave us there to try to figure it out on our own! God provides for our obedience, every single step of the way. In the process, He refines our faith.

As the saying goes, even when we can't see the hand of God (what He's doing) we can trust the heart of God (how He's working).

We have to know the test is coming. If we are not prepared for the test, we are more likely to fail it. Knowing that the test is part of the refining process, helps us to stay focused on the faith journey during the ups and downs of life. The best news is that on the other side of the test, we are going to know God at a deeper level, and we are going to experience His grace in a meaningful way. The test helps us know if we have a fear-filled heart or a faith-filled heart. Are we running to God or away from God?

The truth of the matter is that sometimes we experience both. But every day we have the chance to start fresh by saying, "Lord, today, in the middle of this test, in the middle of this refining process, in the middle of your goodness and grace deepening my obedience and my knowledge of you, I'm going to remain. I'm going to stay put in this testing process. I'm not going to run from it, I'm going to remain in it."

Remaining reminds me of John 15:5. Jesus said, "I am the vine; you are the branches. The one who remains in me and I in him produces much fruit, because you can do nothing without me." When a vineyard owner takes care of his vines, he prunes the branches and twigs so that the vines can bear even more fruit later. It's no accident that Jesus used this analogy because God prunes us in our own process of remaining. He cuts away the things that don't matter (even if we may think they do). He trims away distractions. We may want the easy season of visible growth and success and flourishing...but it won't happen without the pruning in the hard seasons. The more we remain in Him, the more we can bear fruit. We've talked before about how a journey with God offers a chance for sanctification. As noble as 'sanctification' may sound, it's more often a nitty gritty process of becoming more holy, more like Jesus and less like our old sinful selves.

God was teaching and transforming so that in the moment Abraham had an ability to obey. Abraham didn't know that he had that kind of faith until he was put to the test. We need to be able to see the test as a chance to show what we believe about God.

2. Worshiping in the Moment

In the middle of a test or hard season, worship is often the last thing on our minds. We stress about the details or solutions, thinking, "What do I need to do?" "What options do I have?" or even just "How am I going to survive this?" And it's not wrong to try to figure out how to handle our problems. But in order to worship, we have to take our eyes off the details and put them on God instead. This helps us to see the circumstance through God's perspective. Worship challenges the need to change or control our circumstances.

In our Western civilization, we often associate the word 'worship' with
a certain setting (usually a church), a certain mood (happiness or calm), and certain surroundings (everything perfectly organized so we can focus on the music). But at the core of it, worshiping is so much more than music. Abraham certainly didn't have a music band, worship leader, or choir nearby! *Worship—for him and for us—happens when we recognize that God is God and we are not.*

What happens when we worship in the moment? In the hard moments, in the foggy moments, and in the unsure moments, we can show the same attitude as Abraham. Worship invites faith to shape our thoughts, feelings, and actions.

If you are in a situation where you don't know what to do, worship God. If you are in a situation where you're not sure of the next step to take, worship God. If you are in a situation that is hard and you are afraid, worship God.

3. We Walk Up that Mountain

Have you ever had a lump in your throat while you're trying to do the right thing? There's this overwhelming feeling of, "Oh my goodness, this is so hard!" *Hard is hard even when it's right.* It takes endurance and courage to face something that seems impossible; and sometimes, we're just not sure we have what it takes.

When I read about Abraham facing that mountain, I would love to protect Abraham from the moment because I don't want him to have to go through it. But I would never want to take from him what he was about to experience with the Lord. I'm grateful for what he went through and God's heart for him (and us), in seasons of testing. God sees the other side of the mountain. He's calling us to trust Him for the other side.

When Jesus walked up to Lazarus' tomb, knowing his friend had died, He wept. He knew what was going to happen on the other side of that hard moment; He knew Lazarus' story hadn't ended. But He also saw Mary and Martha grieving, and experienced His own human emotions. And Martha told him directly, "Lord, if you had been here, my brother would not have died" (John 11:21). Jesus could have removed every possible 'mountain' of challenge, but He didn't. That wasn't the plan for Mary and Martha and Lazarus, and it wasn't the plan for Abraham and Isaac, and it's not His plan for us either. The heart of God—His intentional plan—is that as we trust Him, we'll get to the other side. There's a provision that keeps us with Him, no matter what—the Holy Spirit. He is our guide, comfort, and help. He gives us the power we need to walk up our mountains by faith.

Whatever we go through, in our hardest moments, God is still the God who sees. He is tender to us. He can do more than we can even ask or imagine (Ephesians 3:20). Whatever you're facing, the power of God is stronger. Our sovereign, providential, purposeful God is going to show up on the scene and provide. He's the one writing our story; He always has been, and He always will be.

4. God Provides the Lamb

We don't always know where God's going to meet us, how He's going to meet us, and how it's going to work out in the process. God's way of providing may not look like the way we want Him to provide. He may give us patience instead of healing, new roads instead of old security, or slow spiritual growth instead of a quick solution. He may turn our trauma into a chance to encourage others, instead of just magically erasing the pain. We don't know what He has down the road for us. But we do know that, when we keep walking by faith, *He will provide.*

The Lord will provide! That's the name Abraham gave to God on the other side of his test. The place of that huge challenge in Abraham's life became the place God sent the greatest provision for his life.

Oh, friend, we have the same story. Our sin represents our hardest moment and greatest challenge. Jesus is our greatest gift. Salvation. That is just one of the ways the Lord provides. Brokenness is real for every single person, saved or not. We live in a world filled with sin, death, and disease. We were never meant to handle our journeys on our own.

It's easy to agree that the famous Abraham had a faith story worth sharing, but what about us? What if we actually kept track of the times God showed up and did something for us? I love the fact that God writes a story with our lives. Our stories are broken, messy, and wonderful all at the same time. There is power in knowing, owning, and sharing our stories of faith. Our stories are made up of spiritual markers that represent important moments. Moments when God provided at just the right time and in just the right way. Moments where we can say, "I know my God, and I'm going to trust my God in this season. I know He's working to write my story in a way I can't see right now."

How can we have confidence in the middle of facing hard moments? How can we trust God in each new struggle? Because God already showed up on the landscape of our lives! God sent His son Jesus to save us because *He is a God that provides.*

Jesus came to this earth. He lived. He died. He rose again. Jesus is the Lamb of God who takes away the sins of this world. We can place our faith in Jesus for the forgiveness of our sins. We can move from spiritual death to spiritual life, and the Holy Spirit can live inside of us. God can show life-changing power through us, especially during the hard moments. Obedient, proven faith, can shape our stories. No matter where we've been, God knows there's always more progress for us to make. We like to avoid tests. We don't want to do the hard things. But there are seasons of life that we can't go around; we have to go through them. On the other side,
we will say, "I saw the Lord. I know God showed up. He provided!"

God is intentional in the way He works and moves. I love that we do not have to wander through our time on this earth, wondering if God sees or cares. We can know He does. Our Savior lives and we can live with abandon for the glory of His name.

Abraham passed his 'big test' in Genesis 22, and I'm so proud of him! As much as some of the 'chapters' in his life may have been more like a warning to us, this chapter holds out hope. This was a picture of someone living **to** God, **with** God, **for** God, and **through** God, even when they couldn't see the outcome. Thinking back on our own lives, we also have had times when we thought God would use us to change the world, only to be disillusioned when it didn't work out like we thought. Or maybe we had times when we just wanted to hide from God's plan for us because we didn't like it or were afraid of what it might demand from us. By journeying with Abraham, we've had the chance to learn (or relearn) that God is oh-so-loving and purposeful, and has a bigger story for us than we can imagine ourselves. And, every step of the way, His grace is sufficient for us. We can trust Him as we journey by faith.

⟫⟫ Transforming Truth:

Trusting God leads to grace in the moment.

"Lord, we love You and we praise You. Thank You for the story of Abraham, Sarah, and Isaac. Thank You for letting us see Abraham's faith being tested and his life being transformed as he followed You. You called this man out of a foreign, pagan land, and You brought him to Your land to be the father of Your people. Lord, we thank You for the picture of obedience we see in the life of Abraham. As we worship in the hardest moments of our lives, we know that You will provide exactly what we need. You are the Lord who Provides!

So God, fortify us in trust. Fortify us in faith. Fortify us in truth to lay our Isaac down. Help us remember that You are fulfilling the plan that You called us to be a part of. John 15 tells us that it is to the Father's glory that we bear much fruit and show ourselves to be Your disciples. Help us to be changed and transformed because we have met with You. In the powerful name of Jesus, we pray, amen."

DISCUSSION QUESTIONS

As we journey through the life of Abraham, think about your life. What is God cultivating in you? How can faith and trust grow in your life? What is your greatest struggle? What is defining you in this season of your journey?

Chapter 9: Grace in the Moment

1. Do you need to be reminded that God sees you, knows you, and loves you? God has a plan for your life; and He has not given up on you!
2. How do you view a test from God? Do you see a purpose in the testing process? Share about a season of testing in your life.
3. We walk up our mountains in different ways. Worship and surrender are always involved in the process. When you face a mountain moment, what do you need to remember about God and His work in your life?
4. Describe the concept of grace. How does grace invite us to trust God at a deeper level? Can you look back over your life and identify moments when God gave you grace in the moment?

This leads to our Transforming Truth: Trusting God leads to grace in the moment.

5. How do you define faith? How has Abraham's story encouraged you in your faith journey? How has your faith grown as a result of studying Abraham's story?

EPILOGUE - BY FAITH

"Now faith is the reality of what is hoped for; the proof of what is not seen. For by this our ancestors were approved."
Hebrews 11:1-2

In the first chapter, we saw the question in Abraham's life, "God can I trust you?" Throughout this book, we see God answering that question over and over again.

I want to ask you a question. As we have walked through the lives of Abraham, Sarah, and Isaac, we've looked at it from the perspective of faith and trust. We've talked about the character, ability, strength and truth of God, and putting our confidence in Him, not ourselves or our circumstances. Here is the question: Have you grown in your faith? Do you trust God more because of our journey together?

Faith is not always feel-good, and it's not always Instagram-worthy. Real faith hangs on in the ups and downs, the twists and the turns, the good and the bad, the beautiful and the not-so-beautiful moments of life. Faith is present in the moment, whether on the mountaintop or in the valley. We need to be reminded of that. Our lives are not always perfect; they're often messy and hard, yet full of encounters with God!

As we've been *On The Road with Abraham*, we've had the chance to develop a stronger faith. From Genesis 12 to Genesis 22, Abraham's faith held on and persevered. It wasn't always pretty, but God was faithful, and Abraham never quit.

Sometimes we can use the reminder that God is faithful in our lives too. God's economy has always been a faith economy, a surrendered economy, a step-by-step economy. It's not always pretty, and it's not always easy. But, it's real, it's deep, it's organic, and it's life-changing. Not only that, the faithfulness of God is experienced during the journey. The ups and downs remind us that God is real and He is present. No matter what, God is worthy to be praised.

What is faith, and how is faith shown in and through our lives? The life of Abraham helps us answer that question. Faith believes that God is real, He has a plan for our lives, and we can trust Him no matter what. (Especially during hard times!)

Faith is not developed in a one-time event. Rather, faith is developed through a process that begins at salvation and continues until Jesus calls us home. Faith is a journey requiring perseverance in the Lord.

If we think of history as a road, the Old Testament is like the very beginning. It tells us about the start of the world, of God's interaction with humans as they struggled with sin and questions. It also points toward the coming of Jesus, with prophecies about the Savior who would come to Israel and the world. The New Testament tells the story of Jesus and the development of the early church. When Jesus came to the earth, He fulfilled every one of the prophecies about the coming Savior. The Bible ends with the promise of Jesus' return and the establishment of God's eternal Kingdom. From Genesis to Revelation, every character, story, and truth reminds us that God is good, He is in control, and His plan will come to pass.

What happens in our past impacts our present, and what happens in our present impacts our future. This is what the journey is—the past, the present, and the future working together, to see the fulfillment of God's plan for our lives. When I read through Abraham's journey from Genesis 12 to 22, I loved seeing how Abraham changed and grew over time. The Abraham of Genesis 12 was not the same Abraham as Genesis 15 and 21! But for him to get from chapter 12 to 22, he had to go through alot in his journey.

As separate stops along the way, Abraham's story isn't very impressive or inspiring. As disconnected years, our stories aren't very impressive or inspiring either! That's why looking at the entire journey matters so much. God is always doing more than we see or know. He is faithful to guide our steps and to prepare us for what is ahead. I can't think of a better reason to trust God and His plan!

In Hebrews 11, a list of faith-filled people is mentioned. I love that Abraham's story is woven in and out of the list. Everyone mentioned in Hebrews 11 lived by faith when their backs were against the wall, and the call of God was big in their lives. If you haven't read Hebrews 11 in a while, give it a read. I recently did, and one phrase jumped off the page at me. The phrase, "by faith…"

This phrase made me stop and think. Abraham showed faith during his journey. Abraham left his homeland and settled in the Promised Land. He entered into a covenant with God and ultimately followed God up the mountain. Abraham was willing to sacrifice Isaac knowing that Isaac was the child of promise. In Genesis 22 & Hebrews 11, we learn that Abraham believed God could raise Isaac from the dead. Talk about living by faith!

Sweet friend, where are you on your journey with God? Where is He taking you from here? I love that our answers will be unique based on God's plan for each of us. But, you know what is the same? *All of us need faith and trust for the journey.* We all have the chance to put ALL of our eggs in God's basket and watch Him do what only He can (and will) do! Thank you for joining me on this adventure. I'm so glad we got to spend some time on the road with Abraham together!

ABOUT THE AUTHOR
Andrea Lennon

Andrea is an "on the go" kind of girl who loves Jesus and shares His message of hope with those she meets. From spending time with her family to speaking at live events, Andrea embraces life and looks for opportunities to grow in her relationship with Jesus.

As the founder of Andrea Lennon Ministry, her passion is to encourage women to know the truth, live the truth, and share the truth. Through speaking and writing, Andrea enthusiastically shares the teachings found in the Bible and helps women apply the Bible to the everyday aspects of life.

Andrea is a 2004 graduate of Southwestern Baptist Theological Seminary. She has written and published Reflecting His Glory: From Conformity to Transformation, Free To Thrive: 40 Power-packed Devotions for Women on the Go, On the Road with Ruth, God in the Window, Hope: More Than A Feeling, and On The Road with Abraham.

Andrea and her husband, Jay, live in Conway, Arkansas. They have two adult sons, Jake and Andrew. Andrea travels extensively and thanks God for the opportunities to meet women, hear their stories, and open God's Word together.

Connect with Andrea online at www.andrealennonministry.org where you can learn about Andrea Lennon Ministry and our three ministry branches: Andrea Lennon Live, True Vine Publishing, and the Girl on the Go Community. Become a Girl on the Go and enjoy an interactive community that loves God and His Word. Our motto is "Know the truth, live the truth, and share the truth!"

Reflecting His Glory
FROM CONFORMITY TO TRANSFORMATION

Reflecting His Glory: From Conformity to Transformation explores Romans 12:2. This study provides a step- by-step approach for you if you long to:
- Recognize conformity in your life.
- Understand the call to spiritual transformation.
- Establish a daily process for renewal.
- View God's will from His holy perspective, not your own.

Join Andrea Lennon as she leads you to discover life-changing truths that teach you how to think like Jesus, act like Jesus, and ultimately reflect Jesus Christ. Come away from this study changed, living for God's glory and not your own.

Free to Thrive
40 POWER-PACKED DEVOTIONS FOR WOMEN ON THE GO!

In *Free To Thrive* author Andrea Lennon presents a clear biblical picture of freedom through 40 power-packed devotions. Each devotion invites you to know and experience God's freedom in every area of your life.

Free to Thrive topics include:
- Embracing God's definition of freedom.
- Viewing sin through the eyes of a holy God.
- Heeding the words of Christ.
- Basing your life on correct theology.
- Fighting a constant fight.
- Doing whatever the Lord asks you to do.
- Passing the point of no return.
- Longing for your real home.

ON THE ROAD WITH RUTH
FAITH FOR THE JOURNEY

Ruth stood on the road between Moab and Bethlehem and considered two very different lives. A life that had been and a life that could be. The choice she made echoes down to our age. Ruth's story is riveting because it is full of heartbreak, loss, and soul-deep restoration.

Daily we stand in the middle of our roads and make decisions that shape our lives. No matter the road that we face, we can know that God is in control and that He has a plan for our lives.

In this book, Andrea shares the story of Ruth. Along the way, she encourages you to examine your own story. Come along on this journey and discover how you can live a life that honors God through:
- Embracing the right set of beliefs.
- Displaying Christ-like character qualities.
- Living with an eternal perspective during uncertain times.

GOD IN THE WINDOW

Do you struggle with letting go of control?

Do you keep God and others at a comfortable distance?

Do you wonder if you can trust God and His plan for your life?

In *God in the Window*, Andrea shares from personal experience how adoption, dyslexia, loneliness, friendship struggles, and lies from the enemy led to feelings of isolation and fear. Thankfully, God stepped in and changed the direction of her story. As you read this book, you will be encouraged to examine your own story as you:
- Ask the tough questions about the challenging circumstances of life.
- See how areas of struggle are limiting and controlling you.
- Begin to experience God's abundant healing and grace.

Hope: More Than a Feeling

If you are struggling to experience hope, you are not alone. Life has a way of being real and revealing what is going on inside of us. Through it all, God has a message of hope for you. You see, at the very core of who God is and how He works, we find hope rising above circumstances, people, and feelings.

Take advantage of the interactive journal at the back of the book, which helps you identify wrong feelings and perspectives to replace them with God's powerful truth! God's message is a message of hope, and it is from His heart to yours. Join Andrea on this faith adventure as we learn how hope is more than a feeling!

BIBLIOGRAPHY

1. "Expect Great Things; Attempt Great Things," *WMCAREY.EDU*, accessed online, https://www.wmcarey.edu/carey/expect/, January 15, 2023.
2. Trent C. Butler, Holman Bible Dictionary, (Nashville, TN: Holman Publishing, 1991), "Abraham," 10.
3. Ibid. 11.
4. "Abraham Facts and Significance," Britannica.com, accessed online, https://www.britannica.com/biography/Abraham, May 15, 2023.
5. David Alexander, Eerdman's Handbook of the Bible, (Carmel, New York: Lion Publishing, 1973), 136.
6. "Ur Shrines & Chapels," Odyssey Adventures in Archaeology, accessed online https://www.odysseyadventures.ca/articles/ur%20of%20the%20chaldees/ur_article05chapels.html, January 15, 2023.
7. Thomas C. Brisco, Holman Bible Atlas, (Nashville, TN: Broadman & Holman Publishing, 1998.), 45.
8. "Abraham Facts and Significance," Britannica.com, accessed online, https://www.britannica.com/biography/Abraham, May 15, 2023.
9. Thomas C. Brisco, Holman Bible Atlas, (Nashville, TN: Broadman & Holman Publishing, 1998.), 45.
10. Ibid. 41.
11. Ibid. "Israel's ancestors came from the peripheral edges of history even though they were at the theological center of God's redemptive plan."
12. Andrea Lennon, On the Road with Ruth, (CreateSpace: Amazon Publishing, 2015), 16.
13. Pat and David Alexander, Zondervan Handbook to the Bible, (Grand Rapids, MI: Zondervan Publishing, 1999), 198-199.
14. "What does the Bible Say About Famine in the Bible?" Got Questions, accessed online, https://www.gotquestions.org/Bible-famine.html, January 15, 2023. "While the physical causes of the famines varied, the Bible indicates that God is in control, even during times of scarcity. God's desire in bringing famine upon Israel was to gain His people's attention in a sure-fire way—through their stomachs."
15. Merriam-Webster's On-line Dictionary, accessed online, https://www.merriam-webster.com/dictionary/consequences, "Consequences," February 9, 2023.
16. "Lies Vs. Truth." Lifeway Women. Accessed online https://women.lifeway.com/ June 15, 2023.
17. J. Vernon McGee, Thru the Bible with J. Vernon McGee Volume 1, (Nashville, TN, Thomas Nelson Publishing, 1981), 62.
18. Ibid.
19. "Abraham Facts and Significance," Britannica.com, accessed online, https://www.britannica.com/biography/Abraham, May 15, 2023.
20. Merriam-Webster's On-line Dictionary, accessed online, https://www.merriam-webster.com/dictionary/trust, "Trust," January 26, 2023.

BIBLIOGRAPHY

21 Merriam-Webster's On-Line Dictionary, https://www.merriam-webster.com/dictionary/preparation, "Preparation." May 16, 2023.
22 "Who was Melchizekek? Got Questions," accessed online, https://www.gotquestions.org/Melchizedek.html, June 16, 2023.
23 The Bible Commands Christians to Tithe, The Gospel Coalition, accessed online, https://www.thegospelcoalition.org/article/bible-commands-christians-to-tithe/, June 20, 2023.
24 Spiro Zodhiates, The Key Word Study Bible, (Chattanooga, TN: AMG Publishers, 1996), #3707, 1521.
25 Courtney Reissig, Promises Kept (Chicago, IL: Moody Publisher, 2023), 18, 36.
26 Hagar: Friend or Foe? Women in the Bible: Exploring Women in Scripture, accessed online, https://womeninscripture.com/2017/07/17/hagar-friend-or-foe/, December 15, 2022.
27 Dick Purnell, Knowing God By His Name, (Nashville, TN: Thomas Nelson Publishing, 1993), 121.
28 Ibid. 24.
29 Zodhiates, The Key Word Study Bible, #5814, 1534.
30 Zodhiates, The Key Word Study Bible, #2556, 1514.

Made in the USA
Monee, IL
12 April 2024